What People Are Saying About A+...

"A+ is powerful. A must read for any parent!"
—Kelly Heaps, Executive Manager
Buckaroo Books

"Each of us goes through periods of cleansing in our lives. Recently, I have struggled mentally concerning my self-worth and direction in life. Being the parent of six children and fifteen grandchildren, plus having a very responsible and demanding career, has put my thought process in overdrive.

After reading this book, I have increased my study into the deep caverns of my mind, and increased my pursuit of living an A+ life.

This information has assisted me by helping me to align my priorities to really be about what is important to me and my family.

Thank you, Wade."

—David R. Hebert, President
North Coast Management, Inc.

What People Are *Still* Saying About A+...

"Wade Cook is an American treasure that gets to the point in a believable and do-able manner. The food for thought presented in A+ can help anyone get going no matter where it is that they are starting from."
—*Barry Knapp, Chief Operations Officer*
Renae Knapp Color Institute Salons

A⁺

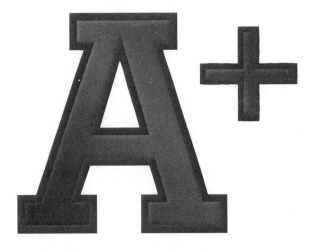

Wade B. Cook

Lighthouse Publishing Group, Inc.
Seattle, Washington

Library of Congress Catalog-in-Publication Data
A+ / Wade B. Cook
p. cm.
ISBN: 0-910019-39-8
1. Success--Religious aspects--Christianity. I. Title.
BV4598.3.C65 1998 248.4--dc21 97-46964 CIP
Printed in the United States of America

All scriptural quotations are from the King James Bible.

Book Design by Connie Suehiro
Dust Jacket Design by Brendan Bigley and Angela Wilson
Photographs by Zachary A. Cherry and Vaughn Tanner

Lighthouse Publishing Group, Inc. a subsidiary of
Wade Cook Financial Corporation
A publicly traded corporation (ticker WADE)
14675 Interurban Avenue South
Seattle, Washington 98168-4664
1-800-706-8657
(206) 901-3100: fax
http://www.lighthousebooks.com

10 9 8 7 6 5 4 3 2 1

To Laura, my wife.

Thank you
for your relentless pursuit
of living an A+ life,
and for being
an A+ person.

Other Books by
Lighthouse Publishing Group, Inc.

Contents

Foreword

Have you ever wondered why some people succeed while others do not? In the simplest terms, successful people act and others don't. Successful people do something every day. Successful people take the initiative; initiative is doing the right thing without being told. Successful people put positive creations into action. Successful people understand and apply the golden rule. Successful people do more than they are asked; they go the second mile.

It has been said that there are three rules for success: go, go on, and keep going. In truth, the only thing that keeps an individual going is energy. And what is energy? It's the love of life. Mark Twain was once asked the reason for his success. He replied, "I was born excited." Wade Cook, like Twain, was born excited. He continues to be excited about life, its many challenges, and opportunities. In his short life he has succeeded in many endeavors. And in his upward climb, he has also experienced disappointment and failure, but through it all he has learned well that success consists not in never falling but in rising every time you fall. Not long ago I asked him for the secret of his success and he said, "It's simple, I never had a job I didn't like."

Wade Cook is the author of thirteen books and three of them have been on the *New York Times* Business Best Seller list. He is recognized as an authority on stock market finances and real estate investments. His company, Wade Cook Seminars, Inc., is a highly successful enterprise in educating and training the public on financial planning and stock market savvy.

He is an outstanding motivational speaker and has written extensively on the art of success. He also has a unique ability to incorporate the wisdom of the Bible in his talks and writings. *A+* is a wonderful example of his genius in blending daily living with the application of the principles of truth found in the scriptures. In this volume, *A+*, he has translated the counsel of Jesus, his own role model, into practical, everyday experiences in life. His art in doing so is somewhat like the story of the four clergymen who were discussing the merits of the various translations of the Bible. One liked the King James Version best because of its simple, beautiful English. Another liked the American Revised Version because it was more literal and comes nearer the original Hebrew and Greek. Still another preferred Moffatt's translation because of its up-to-date vocabulary. The fourth minister was silent. When asked to express his opinion, he replied, "I like my mother's translation best." The other three expressed surprise. They hadn't remembered hearing that his mother had translated the Bible. "Yes, she did," he replied. "She translated it into life, and it was the most convincing translation I ever saw."

Like that minister, Wade Cook has translated the wisdom of Jesus Christ into the language of everyday living. He knows that an individual's true wealth and success are measured by the extension of his influence for good. *A+* will assist all readers in extending their good influence in whatever they seek to do.

—Paul H. Dunn
Author of "Christmas: Do You Hear What I Hear?

Preface

If you've come to *A+* looking for rehashed ideas, or to feel some good warm fuzzies, you're in the wrong book. This book is about living an A+ life, having A+ successes, and finding a ton of happiness, and fulfillment in the process.

When I started writing, I was going to call this book *High Octane Success*. It was not exactly fitting. Then, after the huge success of *Business Buy The Bible*, I was going to call it *Success Buy The Bible*. For months, that was our working title. It was fitting but just didn't feel right. *Peak Performance* was the next title, but this book is about more than that.

I thought long and hard about success and nonsuccess, excellence versus mediocrity, and a host of other topics. I constantly try to live my life "in the second mile," to do more than asked, to be above normal. An A is an A, but what do real achievers do? What do they achieve to get the plus? Is it worth it?

It seems like these questions should be or could be answered simply. But upon reflection, the solutions, and most definitely the processes, do not lend themselves to simple answers.

An A+ life is a phenomenon. Each success is unique, but common attributes pervade them all. Finding and doing these things—these successful characteristics—has been a quest of mine for years. Many people have tried to re-create another Woodstock or Microsoft, or a life like Washington, Lincoln, or Reagan. They can't because pieces of the puzzle of life are put together in a certain way. Successes build upon failure. Trying and testing, problems, hardships, relationships, they add up, and are easy to see in the past tense, but most great people's lives look like diamonds in the rough until they make it. Then like so many in every field of life, after 20 or 40 or 60 years of trying and struggling, they become an overnight success.

My hat is off to them.

I keep searching so I can put my own puzzle together. I found the best role model. He is a carpenter's son, a Jew. He goes by many names. This book will use his most common name, that of Jesus. Though the name be common, there is nothing about his life, his teachings, his actions, his prayers, or his death that are common.

Jesus is a mighty man. His life is worthy of emulation. He alone is the best role model. He lived an A+ life. We can, in our own way, with our own circumstances, do likewise. There are many similar attributes we can develop. We already have the greatest blessing of all—being children of God. He wants the best for us as any loving parent would, and He helps us when we ask.

I wrote this book to help people read God's word, set noble priorities, and be led back to Him. I hope *A+* helps you live an A+ life. I give God the credit for any gain you receive, as "all good things come from the Father." These words are a small token of gratitude to God. They are given to help many read His words, set noble priorities, and be led back to Him.

Life is earnest. Life should be joyful—yes, full of joy. I have found there is no happiness in unrighteousness or mediocrity. Happiness is found in living an A+ life, a life God can be proud of.

Acknowledgments

Who actually goes a third of the way around the world to find great people to work with? I do. Upon arriving home from a trip to Italy, I realized I was back among my team of people who work so hard, with a passion, to keep the company running professionally and smoothly.

One of those people is my fantastic assistant, Patsy Sanders. She is excellent at performing the professional obligations given to her. She handles her job with a positive, professional attitude.

Great employees like Patsy are hard to find, and I am very grateful for them and their faithful dedication to their jobs.

I am also grateful for those in the Art Department who have, once again, finished another book of mine. Mark Engelbrecht, Connie Suehiro, Judy Burkhalter, Angela Wilson, Brent Magarrell, Bethany McVannel, and Vicki Van Hise make up the team of skilled people who design the covers, format the text, and skillfully proofread my books. These employees all get an A+!

In addition, I am forever thankful to my family, especially my in-laws who improve and grow every day. My children are wonderful and keep me grounded; and to my wife, as always, I thank you for being my greatest cheerleader.

Lastly, I must acknowledge God's hand in all things. My gratitude is immense and yet so inadequate compared to His great love for us.

1

The Best Book

I made a statement in a radio ad that "there is in one place a collection of wisdom, thoughts, laws, and principles which could help people make millions, even billions of dollars." This one place is the Bible. Another time I mentioned the wealth of the ancients, and by today's standards, our billionaires do not match up. Many main characters of the Old Testament had land and flocks—riches, as far as the eye could see. Brought forward to our times and adjusted for inflation, you would see how paltry our fortunes are today. I mention this because I've discovered one truth in my search for great financial principles to use and share with my employees, students, and all who will listen. What I have found is simple: if you want happiness, peace, financial prosperity, and a great family, seek out the best principles and the best minds. "To whom are you listening?" has been a constant theme and question asked at my seminars. Yet, it's as if people have given up on the Bible. Do you see it, too? All around us Biblical messages are disparaged. Its concepts are swept under the table in the name of modernism. It is ignored.

The desire to help others discover the wisdom in the Bible, like every other desire in my life, has led to a barrage of criticism, even vehement ridicule. It seems odd, doesn't it? The

1

Bible is there for all to see and read. For the most part, its teachings are easy to read and understand. There is spiritual help in the form of prayer and inspiration, as well as church leaders and Bible schools to help us. It is easy to put to the test. But instead of testing Biblical principles to see if they're true, many people merely mock them, and thus never reap the benefits of Biblical wisdom.

I have tried to follow the Bible. I'm not perfect and have never made a claim to be so. I have said often, "I am a practicing Christian, and I am going to keep practicing until I get it right." My point in bringing this up here is this: why, oh, why do we not use the Bible more? Why do we use it on the Sabbath and not every day? Look at this statement by Woodrow Wilson:

> *There are a good many problems before the American people today, and before me as President, but I expect to find the solution of those problems just in the proportion that I am faithful in the study of the Word of God. I am sorry for the men who do not read the Bible every day; I wonder why they deprive themselves of the strength and of the pleasure. It is one of the most singular books in the world, for every time you open it, some old text that you have read a score of times suddenly beams with a new meaning. There is no other book I know of, of which this is true; there is no other book that yields its meaning so personally, that seems to fit itself so intimately to the very spirit that is seeking its guidance.*
>
> *—Woodrow Wilson,*
> *28th President*

What a wonderful and powerful mini-sermon. Can you imagine anyone in politics today being so bold? And think, when

Woodrow Wilson said it, it wasn't bold at all; it was common, a way of life. Look how far we have strayed from the truth.

For many years I tried to incorporate principles of the Bible into my seminars. I went easy at first, not wanting to offend anybody. I was amazed at the comments. Oh, I got a few people rolling their eyes, but the huge majority commented in word and letter their appreciation for my using these precepts in my business, my lectures, et cetera.

Emboldened by these comments, I actually started quoting a verse or two. I picked logical concepts and showed how they worked for me. I talked about not gleaning the fields in both my real estate and stock market seminars. I told stories of Abraham, Isaac, and Job. From time to time I quoted Malachi and talked about tithing. I told many stories about Jesus—especially the young, rich man, and the ten talents. Usually though, I would rush over them on the way to another point. I did not want to offend anyone. I did not want to turn the seminar into a Sunday school class.

For the most part I still don't. I don't want to be anyone's spiritual advisor. I want to be the best financial educator in America. I am head of a huge, publicly traded company. We have many subsidiaries—including our seminar company. If I were to find a really neat angle on "Writing Covered Calls," my students would want to hear it. I think I've found a really neat angle on living an A+ life and, by judging the thousands of comments, our students want to hear about blending scriptures with everyday business and other activities.

It seems that internal truths strike a common and familiar chord. It's as if our own spiritual lives get disregarded or ignored, or at least out of tune. The ways of the world—greed, selfishness, distrust, and dishonesty—play hard on our souls. They make us feel bad. They are discordant with truthful living. Then, with even a simple scripture, the good feelings come back.

I have never seen anything like the response I have had to *Business Buy The Bible* and *Don't Set Goals.* The comments have been overwhelming and very humbling. It seems some people in this materialistic world just need a nudge to get back to the Bible. That's the point: it is a great book. It has what we need to build relationships, to succeed, to find happiness. God loves us and has given all scriptures for a help in our journey.

Think about it. As you send your kids off to college, or to get married, you write, you phone, and you keep in touch. The Bible, prayer, inspiration, and revelation are God's way of helping us keep in touch while we're away from Him. I know this next part will sound cliche'—the parallel is overused—but think how much better we travel with a good, detailed road map.

I am, at the time of this writing, sitting in Rome. I am not far from where parts of the New Testament were written. I have a good map, and navigating the city is not too difficult. Yet, it would be impossible to find my way without relying on the advice and directions of someone who's already been here.

Yesterday I had an awesome experience. I was able to look back 1,900 years and, for a few brief moments, feel what some early Christians had to go through. They were surely on the road much more than I am. I visited one of 54 catacombs—a labyrinth of caves where Christians were buried—outside the walls of Rome. Many died as martyrs of their faith. They did not have all of the books we now have which make up the Old Testament, and even though they were living when the gospels and other epistles found in the New Testament were written, they did not have them for reading. What we call the Holy Bible came into existence as a collection much later. But what they had, they died for. Simple faith? Yes, but a faith that was a way of life.

Their way of life offended many back then, just as it does today.

People who are trying to do what is best will not always be understood. If you make the Bible important in your life, many in the business community will deride you. Even if you are a famous person, people will sometimes try to make you look bad. Look at the comment made by Earl Spencer, Princess Diana's brother, at her funeral. He could not understand why the press hounded her so and always tried to make the good into bad.

Hopefully, as the Bible precepts come alive, as we let our light shine, some will take heart. Some will be drawn back to God's Word.

Every day for me is a new, wonderful challenge. I want these thoughts in my life. I try to live new scriptures every day. One way for me is to quit hiding and couching the scriptures behind other things. My students' comments strengthened me, and now I have whole seminars using the Bible (especially the covenant of Abraham) as the basis to what I teach. All I am trying to do is get more people to read and apply the Bible—to truly use it, in everything they do.

I have also found this very important for my kids to see. If they see me turning to the Bible often, that example will live with them as they grow older. In management meetings when we are perplexed, we go to the Bible. Never yet have we failed to get an answer. It's almost scary how words from thousands of years ago can be so appropriate today. I know a few of my staff were put off by this use of the Bible, but as far as I can tell, they too have come to appreciate it. There is no proselytizing—just a head-on look at the scriptures for insights.

Tell me a business problem you are having today that Moses did not have. Show me a better system for living than the Abrahamic Covenant—and the better covenant Jesus bought for us (see Hebrews 8). In fact, without meaning to sound crass, show me a better CEO than Jesus.

I am using this first chapter as a way to set the stage for many more chapters on specific things we can do to achieve success. The Bible is a wonderful road map with mighty lessons. We can grow so much by learning from the lives of the ancients.

It is a truly wise person who can see (live) through the eyes of others. Good experiences are the best teacher, but they are so expensive and can cause so much misery. We have faithful Job, competent Ezra, insightful Isaiah, steadfast Daniel, noble leader Abraham, trusting Moses, and hundreds of other prophets and apostles to help us see our own faults and strengths better. The road is so much easier when lighted by such people. The map is sure.

In the end, our successes will be measured by God. If we want success in His eyes, we must know His way—the messages in the Bible will help us achieve success His way.

Here are what other people have said about the Bible:

The Bible is the only source of all Christian truth;—the only rule for the Christian life;—the only book that unfolds to us the realities of eternity. There is no book like the Bible for excellent wisdom and use.

—Sir Matthew Hale

There never was found, in any age of the world, either religion or law that did so highly exalt the public good as the Bible.

—Francis Bacon

The Bible is a window in this prison of hope, through which we look into eternity.

—John S. Dwight

The Bible is the light of my understanding, the joy of my heart, the fullness of my hope, the clarifier of my affections, the mirror of my thoughts, the consoler of my sorrows, the guide of my soul through this gloomy labyrinth of time, the telescope sent from heaven to reveal to the eye of man the amazing glories of the far distant world. The Bible contains more true sublimity, more exquisite beauty, more pure morality, more important history, and finer strains of poetry and eloquence, than can be collected from all other books, in whatever age or language they may have been written.

—Sir William Jones

In what light soever we regard the Bible, whether with reference to revelation, to history, or to morality, it is an invaluable and inexhaustible mine of knowledge and virtue.

—John Quincy Adams

Bad men or devils would not have written the Bible, for it condemns them and their works,—good men or angels could not have written it, for in saying it was from God when it was but their own invention, they would have been guilty of falsehood, and thus could not have been good. The only remaining being who could have written it, is God—its real author. The Scriptures teach us the best way of living, the noblest way of suffering, and the most comfortable way of dying.

—John Flavel

It is a belief in the Bible, the fruit of deep meditation, which has served me as the guide of my moral and literary life.— I have found it a capital safely invested, and richly productive of interest.

—Johann Wolfgang von Goethe

The general diffusion of the Bible is the most effectual way to civilize and humanize mankind; to purify and exalt the general system of public morals; to give efficacy to the just precepts of international and municipal law; to enforce the observance of prudence, temperance, justice and fortitude; and to improve all the relations of social and domestic life.

—Chancellor Kent

The Bible goes equally to the cottage of the peasant, and the palace of the king.—It is woven into literature, and colors the talk of the street.—The bark of the merchant cannot sail without it; and no ship of war goes to the conflict but it is there.—It enters men's closets; directs their conduct, and mingles in all the grief and cheerfulness of life.

—Theodore Parker

The Bible is one of the greatest blessings bestowed by God on the children of men.—It has God for its author; salvation for its end, and truth without any mixture for its matter.— It is all pure, all sincere; nothing too much; nothing wanting.

—John Locke

To say nothing of its holiness or authority, the Bible contains more specimens of genius and taste than any other volume in existence.

—Walter Savage Landor

So great is my veneration for the Bible, that the earlier my children begin to read it the more confident will be my hopes that they will prove useful citizens to their country and respectable members of society.

—John Quincy Adams

The incongruity of the Bible with the age of its birth; its freedom from earthly mixtures; its original, unborrowed, solitary greatness; the suddenness with which it broke forth amidst the general gloom; these, to me, are strong indications of its Divine descent: I cannot reconcile them with a human origin.

—William Ellery Channing

The gospel is not merely a book—It is a living power—a book surpassing all others.—I never omit to read it, and every day with the same pleasure. Nowhere is to be found such a series of beautiful ideas, and admirable moral maxims, which pass before us like the battalions of a celestial army . . . the soul can never go astray with this book for its guide.

—Napoleon Bonaparte on St. Helena

All the distinctive features and superiority of our republican institutions are derived from the teachings of Scripture.
—Edward Everett

Just as all things upon earth represent and image forth all the realities of another world, so the Bible is one mighty representative of the whole spiritual life of humanity.
—Helen Keller

Voltaire spoke of the Bible as a short-lived book. He said that within a hundred years it would pass from common use. Not many people read Voltaire today, but his house has been packed with Bibles as a depot of a Bible society.
—Bruce Barton

I cannot too greatly emphasize the importance and value of Bible study—more important than ever before in these days of uncertainties, when men and women are apt to decide questions from the standpoint of expediency rather than on the eternal principles laid down by God, Himself.
—John Wanamaker

All that I am I owe to Jesus Christ, revealed to me in His divine Book.
—David Livingstone

I have always believed in the inspiration of the Holy Scriptures, whereby they have become the expression to man of the Word and Will of God.
—Warren G. Harding

The morality of the Bible is, after all, the safety of society.
—Francis Cassette Monfort

The Bible rose to the place it now occupies because it deserved to rise to that place, and not because God sent anybody with a box of tricks to prove its divine authority.
—Bruce Barton

That the truths of the Bible have the power of awakening an intense moral feeling in every human being; that they make bad men good, and send a pulse of healthful feeling through all the domestic, civil, and social relations; that they teach men to love right, and hate wrong, and seek each other's welfare as children of a common parent; that they control the baleful passions of the heart, and thus make men proficient in self-government; and finally that they teach man to aspire after conformity to a being of infinite holiness, and fill him with hopes more purifying, exalted, and suited to his nature than any other book the world has ever known—these are facts as incontrovertible as the laws of philosophy, or the demonstrations of mathematics.

—Francis Wayland

Sink the Bible to the bottom of the ocean, and still man's obligations to God would be unchanged.—He would have the same path to tread, only his lamp and his guide would be gone;—the same voyage to make, but his chart and compass would be overboard.

—Henry Ward Beecher

I know the Bible is inspired because it finds me at greater depths of my being than any other book.

—Samuel Taylor Coleridge

Do you know a book that you are willing to put under your head for a pillow when you lie dying? That is the book you want to study while you are living. There is but one such book in the world.

—Joseph Cook

Hold fast to the Bible as the sheet-anchor of your liberties; write its precepts in your hearts, and practice them in your lives. To the influence of this book we are indebted for all the progress made in true civilization, and to this we must look as our guide in the future. "Righteousness exalteth a nation; but sin is a reproach to any people."

—Ulysses S. Grant

The most learned, acute, and diligent student cannot, in the longest life, obtain an entire knowledge of this one volume. The more deeply he works the mine, the richer and more abundance he finds the ore; new light continually beams from this source of heavenly knowledge, to direct the conduct, and illustrate the work of God and the ways of men; and he will at last leave the world confessing, the more he studied the Scriptures, the fuller conviction he had of his own ignorance, and of their inestimable value.

—Walter Scott

One monarch to obey, one creed to own; that monarch God; that creed his word alone. If there is any one fact or doctrine, or command, or promise in the Bible which has produced no practical effect on your temper, or heart, or conduct, be assured you do not truly believe it.

—Edward Payson

There is a Book worth all other books which were ever printed.

—Patrick Henry

I speak as a man of the world to men of the world; and I say to you, Search the Scriptures! The Bible is the book of all others, to be read at all ages, and in all conditions of human life; not to be read once or twice or thrice through, and then laid aside, but to be read in small portions of one or two chapters every day, and never to be intermitted, unless by some overruling necessity.

—John Quincy Adams

A Bible and a newspaper in every house, a good school in every district—all studied and appreciated as they merit—are the principal support of virtue, morality, and civil liberty.

—Benjamin Franklin

The whole hope of human progress is suspended on the ever-growing influence of the Bible.

—William H. Seward

After all, the Bible must be its own argument and defence. The power of it can never be proved unless it is felt. The

authority of it can never be supported unless it is manifest. The light of it can never be demonstrated unless it shines.
—Henry Van Dyke

Nobody ever outgrows Scripture; the book widens and deepens with our years.
—Charles Haddon Spurgeon

A loving trust in the Author of the Bible is the best preparation for a wise and profitable study of the Bible itself.
—Henry Clay Trumbull

I have read the Bible through many times, and now make it a practice to read it through once every year.—It is a book of all others for lawyers, as well as divines; and I pity the man who cannot find in it a rich supply of thought and of rules for conduct.
—Daniel Webster

A noble book! All men's book! It is our first, oldest statement of the never-ending problem,—man's destiny, and God's ways with him here on earth; and all in such free-flowing outlines,—grand in its sincerity; in its simplicity and its epic melody.
—Thomas Carlyle

2

It is impossible to mentally or socially enslave a Bible-reading people. The principles of the Bible are the groundwork of human freedom.
—Horace Greeley

Important Things

Many, many years ago when I was preparing some discussion material for a presentation at a youth conference, I had to do a lot of soul searching. The topic, "Important Things," was one with which I was having a difficult time myself. How could I, as an adult, help these kids when I felt so unqualified? I was to help them get beyond Nike and Calvin Klein. If I could help these youth glimpse something eternal, both in their nature and in the direction they were heading in their lives, even for a few brief minutes, the discussion would be successful. That was a tall order.

Attending would be really great "A" student types, kids who seemed to have it together. Others who hated school and were coerced by their parents to even be at this youth conference would be listening to me. The challenge weighed on me. I was starting to be a success in business and I was starting to use some Bible teachings in my life, but how could I, as weak as I was in the gospel—indeed how dare I—attempt to make these things important to them?

I must have made three different pages of notes and ideas. I was not sure of my approach. Then one day I thought, "Hey, if I am trying to talk of eternal, important things, why not discuss that which is important to God?" I could even start off the discussion that way: "What is important to God?" And if the discussion went well, we could move along to "How do we make these things important to us?"

So to the scriptures I went.

> [35] *Then one of them, which was a lawyer, asked him a question, tempting him, and saying,*
>
> [36] *Master, which is the great commandment in the law?*
>
> [37] *Jesus said unto him, Thou shalt love the LORD thy GOD with all thy heart, and with all thy soul, and with all thy mind.*
>
> [38] *This is the first and great commandment.*
>
> [39] *And the second is like unto it, Thou shalt love thy neighbour as thyself.*
>
> [40] *On these two commandments hang all the law and the prophets.*
>
> *Matthew 22:35-40*

There it was in black and white. Here were enough great ideas and variations on a theme for hours of discussion. My heart raced. Within days I had enough questions and mini-topics that I was worried how to get it all into a 90-minute format.

Like Jesus, let's divide this into two sections: loving God and loving our neighbor. We should not forget the word "like" in verse 39. It seems that these two commandments are closely linked, with love being the foundation.

Before we get into the discussion, may I tell you up front my conclusion? I hope by seeing this first, you will read on and see my reasoning. Here it is: if we want to be happy, if we want to live a fulfilling life, then why not take as important in our life the things that are important to God? It makes sense to me. God created life, so why not live it like he meant for us to? The concept, I think, is sound. Now let's see how we put it to work.

Every action of our lives touches on some chord that will vibrate in eternity.

—E.H. Chapin

Love God

I find it amusing that so many people wanted to trap Jesus. They were always after Him. The trick was to have Him go against the law, either in word or deed. In this type of setting His answers are very specific; they are not embellished (say, with explanations, parallels or allegories). The question is dealt with His way, almost always using answers found in the Torah or original scrolls Jesus had available. The answers were above reproach and above further argument. What we get are short versions of wonderful truths. You know He said more on those topics in other places, but this short answer is remarkable.

"Which is the great commandment?" Obviously this man was familiar with other commandments. Remember, at this time lawyers dealt with the religious laws as there was no major division between the religious and civil laws. They were the same. Why the word "great?" Why not "first," or "most important?" Great, as used here signifies an "umbrella commandment," or "overarching commandment," one to which other commandments adhere or are appendages.

Then Jesus answers, "To love God." In the next verse He calls it a commandment. Why not just put "Loving God" on a recommendation list? No, it is a commandment, and one that you and I had better take very seriously.

To live this commandment we cannot let other things get in the way. No excuses. What we think is important has to be weighed against our desire and actual living of this important commandment. Other things cannot countermand or set aside the command to love God.

Now to make sure there is no misunderstanding, and to make sure our attitudes are right, Jesus adds a few adverbial clauses. (Remember, adverbs modify or explain how and how much. In this case, they add meaning to the verb "love.") The first is "with all thy heart." "With" means in conjunction, or together. "All" leaves no room for doubt. "Heart" has many meanings. It is used to define your being, as in "a team has a lot of heart." It can also mean deep-seated desire, spirit, drive, and indeed the very center of your very existence.

"And with all thy soul." Soul is that spiritual part of us that makes us who we are. It is our spiritual life. Again "all" is used. This leaves no room for anything else.

"And with all thy mind." This one brings to mind, "As {a man} thinketh in his heart, so is he." (Proverbs 23:7) Our minds are amazing. They can think, formulate, rationalize, plan, scheme. What we think about is what we become. I think it is amazing that Jesus wants us to direct our minds to think of God and His ways. What is the alternative? If we wander far it's because our minds are not set on the things of God. Yes, our daily activities are important, but why not involve God—His scriptures, prayers, His ways, all the time? Why be a disciple only on Sundays and thus waste the rest of the week?

Think about it. If Jesus can get us to think about God, not the ways of the world, we will stay on course.

Look at this verse out of Numbers. Balak, an enemy of God's people, has hired Balaam to curse Israel. Balaam tries to curse Israel, but only blesses them. He then tells Balak: "If Balak would give me his house full of silver and gold, I cannot go beyond the commandment of the LORD, to do either good or bad of mine own mind; but what the LORD saith, that will I speak." (Numbers 24:12, 13)

Look at David's admonition to his son Solomon. David should know about complete loyalty. "And thou, Solomon my son, know thou the God of thy Father, and serve him with a perfect heart and with a willing mind: for the LORD searcheth all hearts, and understandeth all the imaginations of the thoughts: if thou seek him, he will be found of

thee; but if thou forsake him, he will cast thee off for ever."
(1 Chronicles 28:9). Please see my comments on the word
"perfect" in *Business Buy The Bible*, pages 35 and 39.

Now we have adverbs and adjectives working together.
A perfect heart and a willing mind should conjure up a certain dedication, excitement, and enthusiasm for the knowledge of God. You might think that behaving this way will
be difficult or full of busy-ness. It is the contrary, though.
Isaiah says, "Thou wilt keep him in perfect peace, whose
mind is stayed on thee; because he trusteth in thee." (Isaiah
26:3)

The more I get into these scriptures, the more impressed
I am. Now we have the word "mind" in the sentence with
"stayed." To stay, or be fixed, signifies permanence. Our
minds are fastened on God. Is this difficult to do? Perhaps,
but not compared to the promises if we do, and the consequences if we don't.

Let me use a few scriptures and tie these thoughts together. We "[receive] the word with all readiness of mind...."
(Acts 17:11) Once the word is received, we become "...trans-
formed by the renewing of your mind..." (Romans 12:2) Each
of us then must "...be fully persuaded in his own mind."
(Romans 14:5)

If we have problems, we can call upon God. We can study
His word, we can associate with others, and we can be
"...with one mind striving together for the faith...."
(Phillippians 1:27) We can even be "...perfectly joined together in the same mind...." (1 Corinthians 1:10)

If we tend to or mind the Lord's business, if our minds
are focused on Him and doing His work, we will find excitement and peace. Indeed our level of spiritual satisfaction
will strengthen *as* we do these things.

Keep Commandments

I think it would be inappropriate to jump on to the second part of Jesus' great answer without exploring a simple

way to love God. Let's go to another question given to Jesus, this time with no antagonism involved. It is the question from the young rich man in Matthew.

16 *And, behold, one came and said unto him, Good Master, what good thing shall I do, that I may have eternal life?*

17 *And he said unto him, Why callest thou me good? there is none good but one, that is, GOD: but if thou wilt enter into life, keep the commandments.*

18 *He saith unto him, Which? Jesus said, Thou shalt do no murder, Thou shalt not commit adultery, Thou shalt not steal, Thou shalt not bear false witness,*

19 *Honour thy father and thy mother: and, Thou shalt love thy neighbour as thyself.*

20 *The young man saith unto him, All these things have I kept from my youth up: what lack I yet?*

21 *Jesus said unto him, If thou wilt be perfect, go and sell that thou hast, and give to the poor, and thou shalt have treasure in heaven: and come and follow me.*

22 *But when the young man heard that saying, he went away sorrowful: for he had great possessions.*

Matthew 19:16-22

I have dealt extensively with this story in *Business Buy The Bible* (page 54-55). There are, however, certain things we should look into here. I'm amazed by Jesus' preliminary questions before he answered this young man's question. He asked "Why callest thou me good? There is none good but one, that is GOD." Wow, the humility, the perspective.

Jesus goes on, "But if thou wilt enter into life...." Let's stop there and go to Proverbs 4:20-27.

20 *My son, attend to my words; incline thine ear unto my sayings.*

21   *Let them not depart from thine eyes; keep them in the midst of thine heart.*

22   *For they are life unto those that find them, and health to all their flesh.*

23   *Keep thy heart with all diligence; for out of it are the issues of life.*

24   *Put away from thee a froward mouth, and perverse lips put far from thee.*

25   *Let thine eyes look right on, and let thine eyelids look straight before thee.*

26   *Ponder the path of thy feet, and let all thy ways be established.*

27   *Turn not to the right hand nor to the left: remove thy foot from evil. (emphases mine)*

I am very amused by the next part of the passage from Matthew. Jesus says, once again in specific response to a question, "Keep the commandments." This could be the Ten Commandments, but it probably means that and more. It likely means all the commandments embodied in the book of laws, the Book of Life.

The young man's next question is just classic, or typical if you think of it. He asks, "Which?" Jesus uses the plural commandments and the ruler uses the singular commandment. It was not only sadly ironic, but sadly pathetic.

My problem with this response is that I can't make fun of it. I also have wanted to pick and choose which commandments to obey. The ruler also wants to pick and choose, or in this case he wants to gain the advantage if he is living the one law he hopes Jesus will state.

Though I have never specifically asked, "Which?," my life and my actions have. When I look at my own spiritual chronology, I, by my actions, asked the same. I knew of the laws. The Bible was on my coffee table. Yet, even when I read this Book of Life, I would pick and choose the commandments which I wanted to live. I usually picked the easy ones, the ones which required very little effort or sacrifice.

Jesus then listed five of the laws he found in the Ten Commandments and added one about loving thy neighbor. The young man stated he lived those, and wanted to know what he still lacked. You'll see by the next two verses that his saying he lived the "love thy neighbor as thyself" part is quite a stretch. "If thou wilt be perfect [again, whole or complete would be a different translation of perfect], go and sell that thou hast, and give to the poor...." (Matthew 19:21) Jesus doesn't stop there, He gives him a wonderful promise, "and thou shalt have treasure in heaven...." Wow, He even asks the young man to come and follow Him.

You know the rest of the story: "He went away sorrowful, for he had great possessions." Great, as you see it used here, as in the Old Testament, means riches. (See **Business Buy The Bib**le, page 14.) The young man tragically let things keep him from getting closer to God.

Love Each Other...

Back to Chapter 22 in Matthew: Jesus had just given the lawyer a specific unarguable response about the great commandment: the first commandment is to love God, and then the second commandment is given. First, Jesus says that the second one is like unto the first. It's as if you can't have one without the other. This is not a hard concept. How can you love God and treat people badly?

"Love thy neighbor as thyself." This is tough. Lord, increase our faith. "As" starts off another adverbial phrase. Love (whom?) as thyself. That should be easy to contemplate though hard to do. We know the attention we give ourselves. We know how much we think about, how much time and money we spend on, and how much we do for ourselves. Do we dedicate the same amount of time and money for others?

While writing this chapter, I happened to discuss this part with my wife. She immediately brought up service to others. We show our love by the service we give. Let's look at another grouping of scriptures. Jesus says:

35 *For I was an hungred, and ye gave me meat: I was thirsty, and ye gave me drink: I was a stranger, and ye took me in:*

36 *Naked, and ye clothed me: I was sick, and ye visited me: I was in prison, and ye came unto me.*

37 *Then shall the righteous answer him, saying, LORD, when saw we thee an hungred, and fed thee? or thirsty, and gave thee drink?*

38 *When saw we thee a stranger, and took thee in? or naked, and clothed thee?*

39 *Or when saw we thee sick, or in prison, and came unto thee?*

40 *And the King shall answer and say unto them, Verily I say unto you, Inasmuch as ye have done it unto one of the least of these my brethren, ye have done it unto me.*

Matthew 25:35-40

Do you see how closely service to others, or loving others as yourself is tied to loving God? If you love God, the Bible says, you'll obey His commands—one of which is to love others. So, loving others becomes a way of loving God.

...As I Have Loved You

The phrase "as thyself" should straightaway help us think about how to love one another, but an added insight is given by Jesus to His disciples shortly before His death.

1 *Now before the feast of the passover, when Jesus knew that his hour was come that he should depart out of this world unto the Father, having loved his own which were in the world, he loved them unto the end.*

2 *And supper being ended, the devil having now put into the heart of Judas Iscariot, Simon's son, to betray him;*

3   *Jesus knowing that the Father had given all things into his hands, and that he was come from GOD, and went to GOD;*

4   *He riseth from supper, and laid aside his garments; and took a towel, and girded himself.*

5   *After that he poureth water into a basin, and began to wash the disciples' feet, and to wipe them with the towel wherewith he was girded.*

6   *Then cometh he to Simon Peter: and Peter saith unto him, LORD, dost thou wash my feet?*

7   *Jesus answered and said unto him, What I do thou knowest not now; but thou shalt know hereafter.*

8   *Peter saith unto him, Thou shalt never wash my feet. Jesus answered him, If I wash thee not, thou hast no part with me.*

9   *Simon Peter saith unto him, LORD, not my feet only, but also my hands and my head.*

10   *Jesus saith to him, He that is washed needeth not save to wash his feet, but is clean every whit: and ye are clean, but not all.*

11   *For he knew who should betray him; therefore said he, Ye are not all clean.*

12   *So after he had washed their feet, and had taken his garments, and was set down again, he said unto them, Know ye what I have done to you?*

13   *Ye call me Master and LORD: and ye say well; for so I am.*

14   *If I then, your LORD and Master, have washed your feet; ye also ought to wash one another's feet.*

15   *For I have given you an example, that ye should do as I have done to you.*

John 13:1-15

So, loving our neighbors as Jesus loved us means serving them, even in tasks as unpleasant as washing their feet.

Jesus lived his life to serve us and even die for us. This is the kind of love we are to give to our neighbors, the love of a life of service.

There are so many lessons to learn here. For all of us, these words may be hard to follow. It is easy to love our friends, people who look and think like us but Jesus tells this story to help us really learn God-like virtues.

3

*The highest earthly enjoyments
are but a shadow of the joy I find
in reading God's word.*
    —Lady Jane Grey

Enthusiasm

When a new business or investment book hits the market, I buy it. I have quite a collection. I constantly look for new ideas, new methods, or little how to's which can make big differences. There are, and will continue to be thousands of management books in the bookstores at any given time. I buy many of them. If I want ideas on agenda planning or meeting structures, or if I want budgeting and cash flow management techniques, I can quickly lay my hands on dozens, if not hundreds, of ideas.

However, in my daily watching and running of my own business (which I feel is superbly successful), or watching other successful businesses, I find something lacking in virtually all of these books. This something—the key to success—is overlooked by authors. This is strange. Most of these authors are successful business *consultants*, and they have missed what made their own business a success. I know because I have talked to them. They are successful because they have enthusiasm, not because of their product or service.

These people come to my seminars. They learn so much in our *Wall Street Workshop* that they themselves are astonished. Many make $20,000 to $30,000 within a month, and then even share my techniques with their clients. Their clients soon come to one of my workshops.

When I find out about their businesses I see several things. One, their businesses are expanding, and they are usually trying to level out the peaks and valleys with steadier cash flow. Two, they have a specialty or a favorite method for helping other businesses. With this method, they are passionate. They have zeal unbounded. They are enthusiastic.

I keep talking to them about how they work with clients. They normally miss the point of what their client truly needs. This key has made them successful but they can't see the trees for the forest. Yes, maybe their new accounting system will help. Yes, getting control of receivables is important. Yes, a better use of floor space will delay the move to a more expensive building. The consultant has done his job by helping cut costs.

Yet, soon other problems arise and the consultant is summoned again. It's a weird cycle and it goes on everywhere. If the owner or general manager doesn't use an outside consultant, he is left to his own devices. The latest trick from a seminar or a cutting-edge management book technique is explored, partially used, and abandoned. But the fix that solves all problems—the cure to the big problem from which all others spring—isn't found.

Band-aids and more band-aids. You've heard that of every 100 business startups, 80% fail within their first year. It's amazing to me that 20% of businesses make it. I am convinced very few people know how to start, run, and build a great business, a business that will support the owner and the owner's kids, not be supported by him or them.

Again, every big-time successful business and every really successful person has the key. Why, again, do so many people miss it? Maybe it's so simple that it's overlooked because of its simplicity. Enthusiasm is what drives a person to take an idea and make a company, and it's that same enthusiasm that makes the company succeed.

Enthusiasm, passion, a love of something, a dedicated drive—call it whatever—it is the single common thread that runs through all success. Enthusiasm is, in fact, sine-qua-non to success.

Nothing is so contagious as enthusiasm.
                              —Edward George Bulwer-Lytton

To see how needed enthusiasm is, how powerful it is, just look at a company or a person's career when they lose their enthusiasm. Look what happens when other things get in the way. Take money for example; is it the living force behind these businesses and people? I dare say, no. Money is nice, but it only drives the attitude a small way. Most gigantic successes love what they are doing.

As a long-time speaker, and as the CEO of a seminar company, I cannot name one other company, either in size or in effectiveness, that matches Wade Cook Seminars, Inc. I personally get hundreds and even thousands of thank you letters and testimonials from customers whose lives have been enhanced in every area because of what we teach.

Yet, if we are good, it is because we love so much what we are doing. My love for helping people and my passion for this business let me tolerate the small negatives. My employees are also passionate and dedicated; they carry the torch well. Our enthusiasm helps us develop innovative solutions to problems that would otherwise bog us down.

Do you think we could have built a half billion dollar company in less than five years (starting with $3,000 and some old office furniture) if we did not love this work?

Look at this verse:

16   *So then because thou art lukewarm, and neither cold nor hot, I will spue thee out of my mouth.*

                                        Revelation 3:16

Can you imagine where we would be if we did not get up every morning excited to improve, to change, to grow, to serve better? We get paid well for our seminars, but the money is not the driving force. I know, at first, it is to some of my employees. But they too eventually come around and get bitten by our dedication to excellence, our passion for sharing and caring, our strong desire to build something that outlasts all of us.

It's catchy. Our customers feel it. Our sales representatives are wonderful. Many make more in the stock market every month than their commission checks. They walk the walk. Very few have quit—even when their income from investments far exceeds their needs and wants. If you ask them why, they usually say they stay because of the excitement. Being around enthusiastic people all day helps them stay enthused in their own lives. Enthusiasm is catchy, and enthusiastic people are exciting to be around.

A few have retired (sometimes they retire two or three times a year!). They keep coming back. I continue to ask why. It's because of the camaraderie and the excitement. The real question for anyone in business or starting a business is this: what can I do to create passion and excitement?

The Greeks put the words "en" (with) and "theos" (God) together to get entheos, and from that we get enthuse and enthusiasm. Yes, a person can be without God and get excited about a track meet, or new product, or a football game. It's usually fleeting though.

What I am talking about is real, lasting enthusiasm. This type best comes from a belief in God, a hope in something beyond this world. Show me a quiet, peaceful enthusiasm, one based on strong values and well-founded beliefs, and I will show you a winner.

This is the type of person who excels every day—who lives his or her life in the second mile, always doing extra. This is the person whose actions continually seek to help and build other people. It is from this type of service that great things happen and wonderful, fulfilling lives are built.

Now, extend this personality to a small group, then to other groups or a larger group, and then to a whole company, and the dynamics of greatness are in place.

I can tell countless stories of companies with and without passion. Remember IBM a few years ago. The morale was low. Inroads by competitors were eating up market share. Sales were down. The stock lost nearly half its value. Some of the best employees were starting up competing companies or going elsewhere to work. It looked hopeless.

I am not privy to things at IBM; I do not know what it was that turned their attitude around. I can surmise. Maybe they had research (new products) too long in the development process. Maybe they needed to get rid of a few bad apples. Maybe they needed one star product or one star salesperson. Turn around they did. After a 2:1 stock split, the stock is four to five times higher. Sales are up. Ads are new and reflect a new attitude. Whatever they did, it instilled a new enthusiasm into the company and greatness (once again) followed. There are thousands of similar examples.

Great Things Don't Happen By Committee

I am going to review an experience I have spoken about in almost every seminar and have written about in almost every one of my books. It is so important to me. It is about seeking guidance.

Remember, even great Abraham went to pay tithes to Melchizedek the priest? Christ sent the healed persons to the priests. Why? I think the answer is found in a marvelous conversation Jesus had with Peter. He told Peter to "feed my sheep" and to strengthen the brethren. Jesus didn't tell Peter to do so whenever Peter felt like it, but when he was converted.

I see a lot of problems, both financially and spiritually, when people seek help from the wrong people. One question I ask at my seminars is, "How many want to make over $100,000 a year?" Almost all the hands go up. Then I ask, "If you want to make over $100,000 a year, why are you talking about making money with anyone who makes under $100,000 a year?" Half the attendees' heads nod in agreement. I add: "To whom are you listening?" Just one formula I teach can help someone starting with $10,000 make $200,000 to $300,000 in the next year. Loaded with enthusiasm, probably caught from me or one of my instructors, they approach their stockbroker or financial planner or even a friend or family member. You know what happens next? You probably do know, because this has more than likely happened to you.

Your newfound idea is shot down, and usually by the flimsiest or stupidest of reasons. It could be a simple, innocent question like, "Are you sure that still works?" It could be a vitriolic attack on the messenger.

It does not matter what the idea is. It will get shot down. Your enthusiasm is a target. Can you imagine, in the furthest stretches of your imagination, your spouse, your friend, your parents, or your stockbroker saying something like this:

"That sounds wonderful, and you're just the person to do it."

"Wow! What a great plan. Let me study up so I can help you achieve success."

"Great! Now go to town and make a million bucks."

Just think of the happiness we would have if we got this response. If you think success is a group affair, think again. Virtually every major change and every great achievement happens because of the passion, the drive, of one man or woman. In the history of mankind, great things do not happen by committee.

It is lonely in these roles. Don't think your friends and family will always understand. They may watch from afar and brag about you if you make it, or point fingers if you don't.

Now if you are on the other side of the fence, and your spouse or friend approaches you, and if you choose to use one of the above responses, make sure their life insurance policy is in force before you do. Remember they may have spent weeks (even years) preparing their presentation. They may have tried to ascertain your negative and naive response and to think up, in advance, their answers to your questions.

It seems like the easiest thing to do in the world is to be critical, negative, or unresponsive. Sarcasm (at this time and any other) serves no purpose. Being negative is the easiest and cheapest way to be. If you're not up to something, you're down on it. Really take time out and consider your responses to others when they have a new idea or plan. Think through the influence you have on others. And then think, "what right do I have to be negative with this person?" Or, "who set me up as judge and jury?"

A case in point: when I wrote my first book on the stock market, *Wall Street Money Machine*, it hit the bestseller list. My seminars took off. Things were great, but I got criticized by the media and some of the financial elite. Stockbrokers everywhere told their clients that my ideas did not work. Much to their chagrin, I suppose, my students persisted. They worked the formulas. Soon brokerages were helping my students learn. They were buying my books and selling them or giving them away. Now, many people tell me that their brokers wait for them to call—to see what they are playing so the brokers can copy them. I have students telling me that when they open a new account their brokers won't let them trade a certain way. They finally say they have been to Wade Cook's Wall Street Workshop; then the stockbrokers welcome them in and allow them to really get going. In just two years, many of my once taboo formulas have become the standard. They're not only tolerated but accepted and used.

Oh, there are still those out there that think I'm on the edge, but they haven't taken the time to really read and understand my cash flow formulas. Bookstore managers tell me they often sell out of dozens of books at a time, because brokers buy my books en masse for their clients. Wow! There is quite a fight going for the paperback rights to both the **Wall Street Money Machine** and **Stock Market Miracles**. Others see the continued sales of my books, and everyone wants in on the success. Where were they when I was being criticized? On the sidelines, like your friends, family, and future partners may be when you tell them the idea you're enthused about.

Things That Work

I am into things that work repetitiously. I look at lives without enthusiasm or at companies lacking spirit, theme, and passion, and I think it's sad.

Give me a man or woman with enthusiasm and we'll set the world on fire. The product or service is secondary. Yes, one can have a passion for his product but the product isn't as important. It's the enthusiasm that endures. An enthusiastic person finds a new or better product. I have always said to bet on the jockey, not on the horse. Now that I have raised, shown, and bred horses, I will add an interesting twist: find a horse with enthusiasm, one that loves to be in the show, and you'll have a winner. There is no substitute for well-directed, sustained passion.

> *Experience shows that success is due less to ability than to zeal. The winner is he who gives himself to his work, body and soul.*
>
> —*Charles Buxton*

A Psalm of Praise

1. *Make a joyful noise unto the Lord, all ye lands.*
2. *Serve the LORD with gladness: come before his presence with singing.*
3. *Know ye that the LORD he is GOD: it is he that hath made us, and not we ourselves; we are his people, and the sheep of his pasture.*

4   *Enter into his gates with thanksgiving, and into his courts with praise: be thankful unto him, and bless his name.*

5   *For the* LORD *is good; his mercy is everlasting; and his truth endureth to all generations.*

Psalm 100

4

I have always said, I always will say, that the studious perusal of the sacred volume will make better citizens, better fathers, and better husbands.
—Thomas Jefferson

Staying Enthused

This book was written on a vacation to Rome. Actually, we made a brief stop in Rome, visited the ruins and the Forum, and spent some time on the Island of Capri. It was a wonderful trip. We met new friends and experienced a very professionally run tour. The trip began and ended in Los Angeles where the majority of participants lived and had some ties to radio station KFWB. (It's a great news station. They deserve a plug.)

The last day, we arose in Capri at 5:00AM to catch a boat to Naples, followed by a flight to Rome, and then at 1:10PM, a flight to LAX (Los Angeles airport). We were to go through Milan and be in Los Angeles at about 6:30PM There is a nine hour difference; it is a twelve plus hour flight. The flight was postponed until 5:30PM—we left after 6:00PM. That five-hour delay put us all on edge.

I wrote a few more chapters. I was going to write two chapters a day in Rome and Capri, but it was so beautiful, and there was so much to do—and after all, it was a vacation.

Most of my books take months to write, but when I write using the Bible as a basis or as a guide I get so excited. The times I spent writing *Business Buy The Bible* and *Don't Set*

Goals were some of the best times of my life. I look forward to these times. I have such a passion for this part of my career.

In Capri, though, I wrote the chapter on enthusiasm. But something was missing. I checked my notes and sure enough, I had missed the part about staying enthused. Keeping up one's enthusiasm is just as important as getting it in the first place. I decided I would write this chapter on the plane on the flight home to Seattle.

We arrived at the gate in Los Angeles about 45 minutes early. I pulled out my pad and finished the chapter "Important Things." I took a stroll into a small bookstore to see if they had my books. They did. I grabbed two *Stock Market Miracles*, opened one, and began to autograph it. I then noticed a young woman, the store employee, and what happened next will seem weird. Well, it was weird.

You see, most bookstore employees will come up and shake the author's hand. They will run and find "autographed" stickers to put on the books. Most will scour the store for other books.

I asked if she had any "autographed" stickers. She saw me signing the book. I introduced myself as the author. This is no joke. She put her forehead down into her hand, almost touching her chest, and shook her head.

I was taken aback. I said, "Don't get so excited." She mumbled, "You come in and just sign the book," and her voice trailed off. She was offended. Maybe I should have asked her permission. Hundreds of other experiences told me store owners and managers were excited to have the books signed. Readers appreciate that the author took the time to sign the book.

She disgustedly walked off. I just left.

A little voice told me, "Wade, you're about to write a continuing chapter on enthusiasm, don't let this affect you." We boarded the plane. I grabbed a piece of paper, took out my pen, and when we reached the taxiway to take off, the electrical system went off. We returned to the gate and had to disembark and take a flight over one hour later.

It was very frustrating. We boarded the next plane, now over a day and a half from Rome, and I was still not home. I sat quietly, trying to collect my thoughts. I looked at my wife and asked, "Would you write this chapter for me on keeping up your enthusiasm? I am having a hard time getting going."

We both laughed. She said, "That's a great start to the chapter—tell this story."

Well, it does get hard to stay enthused. There are so many distractions, so many negatives. I am, frankly, very surprised at how many success stories there are with so much bad, distracting things that seem to rise up to squash good intentions and good works.

I'm not into goals. I don't think that traditional goal setting approaches work. I'm into being the kind of person it takes to be successful. (See ***Don't Set Goals*** for more on this.) *Be* a person who completes things; be a person who measures the cost and is willing to pay the price to complete the task. Don't just say this is a goal and then not live it. The world is full of starters, but is seriously lacking in finishers.

[11]   *Behold, we count them happy which endure.*

James 5:11

Stay The Course

Let me give you ideas from my own life that I hope will help you get and stay enthused.

1. Do your best to understand the cost and the price to pay so you can determine if the effort is worth it.

2. Learn to think and live a life of abundance. (See ***Business Buy The Bible***, chapter three.)

3. Develop personality traits by developing habits of success. The Bible is replete with these.

4. Be careful of your associates' negativity. Yes, Jesus ate with the sinners, but He was Jesus. You can help others and bring them along, but don't let them affect you for the bad. Friendships should build people. Don't get caught up in others' negative way of life.

    Let me say a few more things about who you listen to:

    a. Don't talk to other rookie quarterbacks on how to throw the ball. Talk to the coach. At my seminars I hear people, during the breaks, ask each other questions. I have rarely heard the right answer given. Many people fail because of the bad advice they are given.

    b. Don't give up. Yes, you are a true brother or sister when you help the less fortunate and less deserving, but make sure you charge your own batteries often.

    c. In group discussions, be careful. There is always a tendency for a group discussion to denigrate to the lowest common denominator. One negative comment can destroy hundreds of great comments. Once spoken, the discussion slides into a pit of negative jostling. Remember, it might be lonely, but no great change comes from a committee. It comes from the thoughtful, dedicated, enduring enthusiasm of the "*one.*"

5. Make studying your business. Seek out the best books, with the Bible as your guide. Read. Study.

[1] *Furthermore then we beseech you, brethren, and exhort you by the LORD Jesus, that as ye have received of us how ye ought to walk and to please GOD, so ye would abound more and more.*

    1 Thessalonians 4:1

6. Do not get tied up in minutia. Keep focused on the desired results.

7. Stay healthy. This means to relax and take vacations. Some of us keep the saw working too long. It becomes dull. Take time out to sharpen the saw. The subsequent work will be easier because the saw is sharp.

8. Have a thankful heart. Nothing uplifts and repairs more than being thankful—one who appreciates life and all of its nuances and beauty.

³⁰ *And to stand every morning to thank and praise the LORD, and likewise at even.*

1 Chronicles 23:30

¹ *O give thanks unto the LORD, for he is good: for his mercy endureth for ever.*

Psalm 107:1

9. Remember, things happen when they are supposed to. I love the law of serendipity: find wonderful solutions and happy discoveries on the way to something else.

²⁸ *And why take ye thought for raiment? Consider the lilies of the field, how they grow; they toil not, neither do they spin:*

Matthew 6:28

There is a time and purpose to everything. Find out, by asking God, what He has in store for you.

¹ *To every thing there is a season, and a time to every purpose under the heaven:*

² *A time to be born, and a time to die; a time to plant, and a time to pluck up that which is planted;*

³ *A time to kill, and a time to heal; a time to break down, and a time to build up;*

⁴ *A time to weep, and a time to laugh; a time to mourn, and a time to dance;*

⁵ *A time to cast away stones, and a time to gather stones together; a time to embrace, and a time to refrain from embracing;*

⁶ *A time to get, and a time to lose; a time to keep, and a time to cast away;*

⁷ *A time to rend, and a time to sew; a time to keep silence, and a time to speak;*

⁸ *A time to love, and a time to hate; a time of war, and a time of peace.*

Ecclesiastes 3:1-8

10. Don't ever, ever, ever give up. Endure things well. Stay strong. Walk uprightly. Not every road is a winner. Try and try again. It might take 10 to 50 years to be your own overnight success, but stay true, stay focused, and stay the course.

11. Involve God and family in all you do. Seek Him out in all things. Pray. Ponder. Meditate. Surround yourself in business with your family. Build a family dynasty within a Godly framework. Don't get so busy that you lose sight of things eternal.

Well, that wraps it up. It's time to go be with my kids. The trip was wonderful. Like most things in life, there were the good and bad. I arrived home with this chapter complete and with this book almost finished. There were a few references I needed to check when I got to my more extensive library at home, but my enthusiasm was back in line, and my path clearer. In fact, it continues to become clearer every day.

Please consider my admonitions throughout this book to read and use the Bible more often. It's a great source to keep your enthusiasm level high.

5

The grand old Book of God still stands, and this old earth, the more its leaves are turned over and pondered, the more it will sustain and illustrate the sacred Word.

—*Professor Dana*

Hands

And, Thou, LORD, in the beginning hast laid the foundation of the earth; and the heavens are the works of thine hands.

Hebrews 1:10

When I was but a boy, we often sang a song in Sunday school. It went like this:

I have two little hands folded snugly and tight,
They are tiny and weak but they know what is right.
During all the long hours till daylight is through,
There is plenty indeed for my two hands to do.

I know it seems simple, but these words are true. There is plenty to do indeed, and there are very meaningful things to accomplish. In all times past, virtually every job or career required the use of one's hands. Artists, carpenters, masons, farmers, shepherds, painters, even philosophers and theologians used their hands to work. Hands were meant to be busy. They were not meant to be idle.

Look at your hands. The fingers, the muscles, fingernails, nerve endings, the power to grip, the ability to hold many things; your hands are complex tools. Look at the gestures that the hand can make. Look at the work they can do.

Those of us who have lost the use, even temporarily, of our hands know how awkward life can be. Simple tasks, such as tying a shoelace or buttoning a shirt, become ominous. Often we have to ask for help—indeed, we need to use someone else's hands. Even a cut or sprain of the tendons or ligaments can make you see the importance of a thumb or index finger. You quickly realize how important such a small part of the body can be.

I am awed by all of the body. The hand is no exception. If one robot could do the myriad work and function of our hands, it would be so advanced as to seem a miracle. The hand is so biologically complex that it can perform both heavy and delicate tasks. If it weren't so common, it would be a miracle. Still, I like to think of our hands as a precious gift from God.

The hands are meant to be busy. It seems to me that when the hands are busy, even doing repetitious or mundane things, it gives the mind time to think in different ways. It's the link between our voluntary and involuntary nervous systems. It's a link that most of us pass up, or surely don't utilize to the fullest.

The mind can do wonderful things. It can think up new ideas, innovate, solve problems, and plan out solutions. For me, this is often done when I am busy with my hands. I know this sounds crazy, but I used to love washing dishes by hand, especially when I could be alone. Usually, a ten-minute job would go on for about an hour. I would play in the water—the bubbles, the pans, the upside-down jars with water, and air in and out. I did not consciously stay at the sink; my mind got lost in the process. It was a relaxing time. I cannot now pinpoint any earth-shattering invention or great solution, but I know the process helped me.

I have experienced the same thing gardening and working with wood. I'm not much of a mechanic, but I love working on machines. I get the same high with all types of hand-to-hand busy-ness. Maybe it's one of the reasons I like to drive. I know that my hands are not that busy, but other body parts are—eyes and ears especially. I can drive for hours. If I have a ways to go, I take a pad or a single piece of paper for notes. My management meetings, seminars, and recording sessions are planned while I'm driving. My problem is that I like rock-and-roll too much. If I turn off the radio and let my mind go it can be an awesome experience.

The only movement better for me is walking. As I look at history, it seems to me that virtually every major "thinker," including Jesus, walked a lot. I know they did not have the forms of transportation that we have, but think of the great truths that came from them. Even today, people who walk and exercise a lot have an edge over those who do not. I've had countless people extol the virtues of walking. I know the spinal column needs movement (especially from the base) for the proper flow of fluids. I know that to keep weight off, fat has to be burned, and the fastest way to do so is to use the largest of muscles, the thigh muscle. I know while walking, it is also easy to develop other muscles with simple exercises. I also know that to fill our eyes, nose, and ears with the beautiful things God has given us, walking is fulfilling in and of itself. But this I also know: when we are busy walking, using our hands and legs in repetitious movements, our minds are let free to be creative and enjoy good feelings.

Deuteronomy 3:24 says:

24 *O LORD GOD, thou hast begun to shew thy servant thy greatness, and thy mighty hand: for what GOD is there in heaven or in earth, that can do according to thy works, and according to thy might?*

I will even take it one step further. Walking or being busy with our hands may be a foot in the door for God to get into our lives and make a difference. After all, He gave us these remarkable bodies, should He not know how to reach us? We just need to get ourselves in a position for this communion. It can be at church, at choir practices, while rocking a baby back to sleep, in humble prayer, or out for a stroll or brisk walk at sunrise or sunset.

As I wrote this chapter, I was sitting in the lobby of the Hotel Quisisana on the Island of Capri, just off Naples, Italy. I had come down at 5:30AM, because I awoke thinking of this book. I prayed for inspiration and it came like a flood: I thought about hands. I wanted to walk with a group of newly found friends at 7:00AM. This gave me an hour and a half to get into my typical word search book and look up "hands."

I found several wonderful scriptures, but the feelings I had were simple. Many people in this fast paced society need to use their hands and legs once again. Even if it means back to basic, mundane things, there is a peace, a creativity, a rejuvenation that comes from using our hands and hearts in sync. God has so much in store for us, but we get so busy we fail to take advantage of these opportunities—we let them pass by.

Let me tell about something I do personally. Lately I've put out quite a few books. I feel a big part of me is in the expressions I make while writing. I've never considered myself an author, and I know much of what I write is hard to muddle through. If there is anything really good it is because of good editors and proofreaders.

I am often asked how I write—what method I use. When I tell people I grab a good pen and pad and start in, they are sometimes astonished. How can I use such an old system when word processing programs and dictation machines are available? I have tried all of those methods and still I prefer the longhand writing method. I know it takes longer, but it works. I've dictated many hours, however, and it seems it takes longer to edit what was then transcribed than to write longhand in the first place.

Let me explain what happens. When I'm writing, when my hands are busy, and simultaneously one part of my brain is semi-concentrating on what I am doing, bam, a thought enters my mind. It could be an add-on to what I'm writing, a story, a scripture, or an off-the-wall idea. I have no idea where these come from. I've learned to immediately stop what I am doing and write notes in the margin or, if the idea occurs to me elsewhere, write it on a separate pad.

The ideas come so fast, so powerfully, yet so fleetingly that I must write them post haste. I've learned that I can always pick up my train of thought on what I was writing—I have a sentence or even a paragraph to refresh my memory. (It happened as I wrote the word "refresh." I've wanted to explore the prefix "re" and all the words it changes. But elsewhere. It's now in my notes, and I can go back to my thought any time). If I fail to act quickly, even if I think I can make it to the end of the sentence, I'll forget—and the new thought is usually gone forever. I wish I had more time to research this phenomenon. I'm sure there are scientific explanations of how the brain works when the body is doing something else.

Work Of Our Hands

> [17] *And let the beauty of the Lord our God be upon us: and establish thou the work of our hands upon us; yea, the work of our hands establish thou it."*
>
> *Psalm 90:17*

Let's turn this around. The work of our hands is to be established, or set right, and we are the work of His hands.

> [8] *But now, O Lord, thou art our father; we are the clay, and thou our potter; and we all are the work of thy hand.*
>
> *Isaiah 64:8*

Our hands are but extensions of our hearts. They perform the work thought up in our hearts and minds. Surely we must be about good.

4   *He that hath clean hands, and a pure heart; who hath not lifted up his soul unto vanity, nor sworn deceitfully.*

5   *He shall receive the blessing from the* LORD, *and righteousness from the* GOD *of his salvation.*

Psalm 24:4, 5

6

The word of God will stand a thousand readings; and he who has gone over it most frequently is the surest of finding new wonders there.

—James Hamilton

For Your Words

All of us, I am sure, have spoken words of praise, gratitude, and kindness. Likewise, from the same tongue can come evil, unkind, and inappropriate words.

Just as both good and bad can come from the same mouth, that which comes out of the mouth entered my mind as I began to write this chapter. For this discussion, again, I will stay with the good side of this topic. But don't forget, "a tongue is only a few inches long but can kill a man six feet high," and words sometimes commit us to a path we should not be on.

I believe it is essential to say out loud proper words. We can learn and choose words of power, words that uplift, inspire, and set things straight.

Let's speak of two lovers. They meet, date, and court. Even if they fall in love by looks only, their thoughts and dreams are described in words. It would be unthinkable for two to get married and share a life together if they can't communicate, and most communication is expressed in words.

I know all the body-language people just jumped up in defiance, and the intuitive people want to get their two cents in, but think about it. It is talking that helps people fall in love. It is also talking badly or not talking that causes some people to fall out of love.

Talking kindly and romantically helps people stay in love. Angry and short tempered statements ruin the mood of any event. Just as we can't imagine a relationship with a person without talking, try to imagine building a relationship with our Creator without talking. And I mean talking out loud. I know God knows our every thought, and I'm aware of times when a silent prayer is needed, but there is power in the spoken word.

When Jesus was asked how to pray he said, out loud, the following:

9   *After this manner therefore pray ye: Our Father which art in heaven, Hallowed be thy name.*

10   *Thy kingdom come. Thy will be done in earth, as it is in heaven.*

11   *Give us this day our daily bread.*

12   *And forgive us our debts, as we forgive our debtors.*

13   *And lead us not into temptation, but deliver us from evil: For thine is the kingdom, and the power, and the glory, for ever. Amen.*

Matthew 6:9-13

I could write a book on this prayer but my point is simple: He raised His voice in prayer.

Now, let's explore the story of Daniel. I love this story. He was put to the test several times. His life and the lives of his friends were put in danger. The third time that he was under fire, he needed divine intervention and a being appeared to him.

The others with him felt a quaking but they did not see the man. They ran and hid.

8   *Therefore I was left alone, and saw this great vision, and there remained no strength in me: for my comeliness was turned in me into corruption, and I retained no strength.*

⁹ *Yet heard I the voice of his words: and when I heard
the voice of his words, then was I in a deep sleep on
my face, and my face toward the ground.*

¹⁰ *And, behold, an hand touched me, which set me
upon my knees and upon the palms of my hands.*

¹¹ *And he said unto me, O Daniel, a man greatly beloved, understand the words that I speak unto thee,
and stand upright: for unto thee am I now sent.
And when he had spoken this word unto me, I stood
trembling.*

Daniel 10:8-11

And now to the point. Daniel had raised his voice. He
asked for things and heard the message. Then this heavenly
visitor said to him:

¹² *Then said he unto me, Fear not, Daniel: for from
the first day that thou didst set thine heart to understand, and to chasten thyself before thy God,
thy words were heard, and I am come for thy words.*

Daniel 10:12

May I ask you to read that last verse again? This vision
did not just happen. If his heart had been wrong or if he
hadn't been repenting, this most likely would not have happened, but he was doing those things. The lesson of this is
that his words were right, and he received yet more knowledge. The story gets better, and I'm confident it points to
our time. I encourage you to read all of Daniel. It's a powerful story of faith, endurance, and loyalty.

Note: in the Torah the word "word" is translated as
"prayer." "I am come for thy prayers." It's the words of our
prayers that need to be spoken. God listens to our words.

What About You?

Let's say you read this and think, "Okay, it was this way
with Daniel, but I don't know what to ask for." Then follow

Jesus' example first: reread the Lord's prayer. If you have specific needs or desires and you don't know how to ask for them, then your prayer should request that God help you find the words. Say a prayer on how to be taught to pray. Simply ask God to put the words in your mouth or mind. I can't imagine Him turning anyone away. As you continue, your words will get better.

Words Get Better

I've noticed in my own life and in the lives of hundreds of people that as they mature toward God and speak often of Godly or spiritual things, the quality of their language improves. It almost gains a melodic or singsong quality. Often it borders on poetic.

I know some of this comes by way of two avenues. They either abandon raunchy words, or they fill the vacuum with words, phrases, and thoughts gained by reading better books, including the Bible.

Do you remember the story of Peter who, when accused of knowing and being with Christ, denied it three times. Even though he did deny it, his accuser said, "...thy speech bewrayeth thee." (Matthew 26:73) His words gave him away. Think of our own lives; our speech does betray us.

There are many talkers but few achievers. If you've read **Don't Set Goals,** you know how I detest the old New Year's resolution type of goal setting—"I'm going to lose weight." It's usually fruitless, but people are nearly professional about their method of convincing others of their good intentions.

Talking here should only be after the feat—or after determining the priorities, calculating the method to be used and the price to pay, and building up the resolve necessary to finish. Completion is more important than the start. Don't let words get in the way.

Speak out loud your target. Say it out loud. Raise your voice. Be your own coach. Say the right words; say them often; say them with passion.

Make No Excuses

When something goes wrong, be quick to acknowledge it, make changes, and get going again. The world is full of excuse makers—at this some people excel. They get an A+, but this A+ is for doing the wrong thing. Again, to the Bible we go. When Jesus was on the cross, people treated him so cruelly. He had power to forgive. He could have made all kinds of excuses for these wicked people. He made no excuses, he didn't worry about their upbringing or lack of social graces. He simply forgave them: "Father forgive them, for they know not what they do." (Luke 23:34) Why do we spend so much time in this wasteful area of making excuses? Making excuses makes no sense.

I must tell you about Pat. She came to my real estate seminar years ago. At the age of 72, she became very successful. She stood up in a seminar and almost took the event away from me. She told her story. She made lots of money using my methods. She then looked at all the attendees and said, "You can make money or you can make excuses, but you can't make both." Hear, hear.

Whining, sniveling words serve no purpose. Garnish your thoughts with beautiful God-like ideas. The right words will come.

The effective use of words spoken in a timely, patient manner are pebbles placed rightly in our path of life. Don't miss the growth that will come as you express better thoughts—in both words and actions.

7

The greatest humbug in the world is the idea that money can make a man happy. I never had any satisfaction with mine until I began to do good with it.
—*C. Pratt*

Wealth

This chapter will be about making money. We'll put under a microscope our businesses and careers and see if we can achieve financial success using Biblical principles and methods.

"Is it a sin?" will be our point of reference. Is it a sin to be poor or rich? Is God blessing some and punishing others? Are we in control or out of control of the process? Can we create wealth by not relying on God? Are there direct blessings from certain actions?

Every time I hear these questions, I come to realize how perplexing money is. You're blessed if you're rich, but riches are a curse. There is much confusion on the matter. If the financial books and even the self-help books broach these questions, the answers are far-fetched or boil down to a few admonitions by the author, and then they usually end with this: "you'll just have to figure it out for yourself."

I don't see such confusion if one goes to the Bible. There are clear answers to these questions and more.

> 18 *But thou shalt remember the LORD thy GOD: for it is he that giveth thee power to get wealth, that he may establish his covenant which he sware unto thy fathers, as it is this day.*
>
> *Deuteronomy 8:18*

No, it is not a sin to be rich or poor. Wealth is actually neutral. It is not good or bad. It just is. Now our actions, both in the getting and the owning (stewardship) of wealth, are suspect.

> 33   *But seek ye first the kingdom of GOD, and his righteousness; and all these things shall be added unto you.*
>
> *Matthew 6:33*

It comes down to this. God wants us to think of Him often. He wants our love and devotion. He wants us to have no other gods—including money. He, however, loves us and wants to give us all He has. He wants to bless us in ways we can't even imagine.

> 4   *For since the beginning of the world men have not heard, nor perceived by the ear, neither hath the eye seen, O GOD, beside thee, what he hath prepared for him that waiteth for him.*
>
> *Isaiah 64:4*

> 9   *But as it is written, Eye hath not seen, nor ear heard, neither have entered into the heart of man, the things which GOD hath prepared for them that love him.*
>
> *1 Corinthians 2:9*

He wants us to prosper.

> 27   *Let them shout for joy, and be glad, that favour my righteous cause: yea, let them say continually, Let the LORD be magnified, which hath pleasure in the prosperity of his servant.*
>
> *Psalm 35:27*

He has set up rules for us to live by. Simple things like the following:

¹⁴ *Thou shalt not oppress an hired servant that is poor and needy, whether he be of thy brethren, or of thy strangers that are in thy land within thy gates:*

¹⁵ *At his day thou shalt give him his hire, neither shall the sun go down upon it; for he is poor, and setteth his heart upon it: lest he cry against thee unto the* LORD, *and it be sin unto thee.*

Deuteronomy 24:14, 15

¹⁵ *Ye shall do no unrighteousness in judgment: thou shalt not respect the person of the poor, nor honour the person of the mighty: but in righteousness shalt thou judge thy neighbour.*

Leviticus 19:15

³⁵ *Ye shall do no unrighteousness in judgment, in meteyard, in weight, or in measure.*

Leviticus 19:35

²¹ *When thou gatherest the grapes of thy vineyard, thou shalt not glean it afterward: it shall be for the stranger, for the fatherless, and for the widow.*

Deuteronomy 24:21

Most of these laws have a relationship element to them. He is concerned how we treat each other. He is offended by greed and when we treat another of His children rudely or unjustly.

In the economy of Heaven there is no wasted time. Because of this, God wants us to get our lives in order. To do so, we must accept personal responsibility for our actions. To help us, we need a clear understanding of our responsibilities. We need to know what He expects from us. To do this, He has established covenants—or two-way promises. "I'll do this if you'll do that," would be a simple covenant. The greatest covenant of ancient times was given to Abraham.

It is the basis for God's dealings with man. There are promises of prosperity if we will be His people and walk uprightly in this covenant. The prime covenant is laid out in Genesis:

> 7 *And I will establish my covenant between me and thee and thy seed after thee in their generations for an everlasting covenant, to be a GOD unto thee, and to thy seed after thee.*
>
> 8 *And I will give unto thee, and to thy seed after thee, the land wherein thou art a stranger, all the land of Canaan, for an everlasting possession; and I will be their GOD.*
>
> 9 *And GOD said unto Abraham, Thou shalt keep my covenant therefore, thou, and thy seed after thee in their generations.*
>
> *Genesis 17:7-9*

God's dealings with man in those times were within the bounds of the covenant. Christians believe Jesus made us partakers of this covenant and even established a better covenant, with better promises.

> 6 *But now hath he obtained a more excellent ministry, by how much also he is the mediator of a better covenant, which was established upon better promises.*
>
> 7 *For if that first covenant had been faultless, then should no place have been sought for the second.*
>
> 8 *For finding fault with them, he saith, Behold, the days come, saith the LORD, when I will make a new covenant with the house of Israel and with the house of Judah:*
>
> 9 *Not according to the covenant that I made with their fathers in the day when I took them by the hand to lead them out of the land of Egypt; because they continued not in my covenant, and I regarded them not, saith the LORD.*

> ¹⁰ *For this is the covenant that I will make with the house of Israel after those days, saith the LORD; I will put my laws into their mind, and write them in their hearts: and I will be to them a GOD, and they shall be to me a people:*
>
> ¹¹ *And they shall not teach every man his neighbour, and every man his brother, saying, Know the LORD: for all shall know me, from the least to the greatest.*
>
> ¹² *For I will be merciful to their unrighteousness, and their sins and their iniquities will I remember no more.*
>
> ¹³ *In that he saith, A new covenant, he hath made the first old. Now that which decayeth and waxeth old is ready to vanish away.*
>
> *Hebrews 8:6-13*

Abraham, Isaac, Jacob, Joseph, Job, and all the others knew of and fought to be in this covenant. I'm humbled when I read of Joshua. Moses died and Joshua took over. He worked with the people, but they had erring ways. Probably one of the greatest challenges ever asked is this: "Choose ye this day whom ye will serve...as for me and my house, we will serve the LORD." (Joshua 24:15) I see this scripture in paintings and plaques in many Christian homes.

The rest of the chapter is so poignant that I thought I'd add it here to give depth to this discussion.

> ¹⁹ *And Joshua said unto the people, Ye cannot serve the LORD: for he is an holy GOD; he is a jealous GOD; he will not forgive your transgressions nor your sins.*
>
> ²⁰ *If ye forsake the LORD, and serve strange gods, then he will turn and do you hurt, and consume you, after that he hath done you good.*
>
> ²¹ *And the people said unto Joshua, Nay; but we will serve the LORD.*

²² *And Joshua said unto the people, Ye are witnesses against yourselves that ye have chosen you the L*ORD*, to serve him. And they said, We are witnesses.*

²³ *Now therefore put away, said he, the strange gods which are among you, and incline your heart unto the L*ORD *G*OD *of Israel.*

²⁴ *And the people said unto Joshua, The L*ORD *our G*OD *will we serve, and his voice will we obey.*

²⁵ *So Joshua made a covenant with the people that day, and set them a statute and an ordinance in Shechem.*

²⁶ *And Joshua wrote these words in the book of the law of G*OD*, and took a great stone, and set it up there under an oak, that was by the sanctuary of the L*ORD*.*

²⁷ *And Joshua said unto all the people, Behold, this stone shall be a witness unto us; for it hath heard all the words of the L*ORD *which he spake unto us: it shall be therefore a witness unto you, lest ye deny your G*OD*.*

²⁸ *So Joshua let the people depart, every man unto his inheritance.*

Joshua 24:19-28

Note how the Israelites so desperately wanted to be accepted by God. Joshua pushed them away. It was a test of wills. With God it is always such a test: to see if we will serve Him at all costs. The covenant of Abraham deserves much study and attention.

Try Something New

Most people reading this have probably started and failed at several enterprises. I have, too. Not until I made an effort to employ the wisdom of those smart people of the past did I truly start to prosper. Day in and day out I found new scriptures to live by, and I try to get better at the ones I already know. It's as if a floodgate was opened.

Now when people ask me how to get rich, I say, "study the Bible." It's wonderful in its depth and scope. It's so mesmerizing. I will dare say you can't find one problem today for which there are not answers in the Bible.

So what is needed is a start and a resolve to learn and use these wise lessons out of the past. Let me give several hints to get you going.

1. Start by rereading the covenant. It can be found in Genesis, chapter 17.

2. Study 1 Chronicles 16:15-17:

   15 *Be ye mindful always of his covenant; the word which he commanded to a thousand generations;*

   16 *Even of the covenant which he made with Abraham, and of his oath unto Isaac;*

   17 *And hath confirmed the same to Jacob for a law, and to Israel for an everlasting covenant.*

3. Then read its effect on Isaac in Genesis 26:13.

4. Read Leviticus, chapter 19. This is an awesome book. There are a lot of daily how-to's. This chapter is called the book of holiness. It is the book the Jews read on the afternoon of Yom Kippur.

5. Learn the power of formulas—cause and effect. Start with Psalm 119. It gets a little redundant, but read how much David loved the laws, the statutes, and the commandments. Then in your business figure out the methods, the processes, and the formulas that bring continued success.

6. Study the Be-attitudes. Read them often. Actually read all of Matthew 5, 6, and 7. Many characteristics for building great relationships are there, and the most important is specific advice on how to build a relationship with God.

7. Think of God often. Pray often. Carry a Bible with you. Read it at red lights while you're waiting. You don't have to worry about the light turning green, the guy behind you will honk.

8   *This book of the law shall not depart out of thy mouth; but thou shalt meditate therein day and night, that thou mayest observe to do according to all that is written therein: for then thou shalt make thy way prosperous, and then thou shalt have good success.*

Joshua 1:8

8. Get yourself in an improvement mode. It's tough to circumspectly look at your attitude, your actions, and the changes you're making. Quit trying to change others.

These laws have been very important to me. As I get older they become increasingly so. Oh, how I wish I could reach the teenagers and people in their twenties and thirties. Some get it, but most don't. They are so busy picking and choosing their own paths that they fail to grasp the truly important formulas for wealth and happiness. I wrote extensively about these riches in **Business Buy The Bible**. If you like these methods, I commend you to that book.

Now run your business or your life based on good values. Don't compromise here. A person of integrity is a worthy person to become. God's laws work. He will bless you if He chooses.

Work with your staff and family to make these principles come alive (never preach). Dishonesty will go down; great ideas will come up. You and the people around you will be happier and more energetic—and you will live your lives with more passion.

8

Scholars may quote Plato in their studies, but the hearts of millions will quote the Bible at their daily toil, and draw strength from its inspiration, as the meadows draw it from the brook.
—Moncure Daniel Conway

Be Happy

When asked what makes people happy, there are many responses. When the question is changed to "What makes people unhappy, or what stops happiness?" the answer focuses in on a few key feelings. Fear makes us unhappy. Fighting also brings unhappiness. So does feeling unworthy or unfulfilled, or even feeling nonproductive.

I am confident that God wants us to be happy. He wants us to find joy and peace. The Bible and almost all other books of good report share ways to find happiness. Few deal with how to stay that way. We'll cover that later.

I'd like to share my take on this important topic. You won't find here the typical stuff on happiness. The first and foremost advice I'll give is that we need to want to be happy. We need to dedicate ourselves to the pursuit of happiness.

The best place to start is to stop being unhappy. I know that sounds simple. All it takes is a small shift in our thinking process. Let me get personal with you. Recently I had a birthday. I figure I'm halfway through my life. The first half has been an awesome experience. I have notches on my belt anyone would be proud of. I have a loving wife and a wonderful family. I have honored friends and a great business. By all worldly standards I am successful.

But, as of late, I have been unhappy. Actually, upon look-ing back, I see many years of not being as happy as I could have been. I felt frustrated. It seemed hard to accept the de-mands and act within the different capacities thrust upon me. I must have wanted to be busy, or I wouldn't have cre-ated all this busy-ness. I felt put upon by some people—friends and employees. I was becoming a petty manager, too.

I didn't want to be this way—life wasn't all that fulfill-ing. Some days, I'd wake up happy, and before I got to the office, I'd be upset. There was no call for this. I was blessed beyond measure. Then I reread Psalm 145.

1 *David's Psalm of praise. I will extol thee, my God, O king; and I will bless thy name for ever and ever.*

2 *Every day will I bless thee; and I will praise thy name for ever and ever.*

3 *Great is the Lord, and greatly to be praised; and his greatness is unsearchable.*

4 *One generation shall praise thy works to another, and shall declare thy mighty acts.*

5 *I will speak of the glorious honour of thy majesty, and of thy wondrous works.*

6 *And men shall speak of the might of thy terrible acts: and I will declare thy greatness.*

7 *They shall abundantly utter the memory of thy great goodness, and shall sing of thy righteousness.*

8 *The Lord is gracious, and full of compassion; slow to anger, and of great mercy.*

9 *The Lord is good to all: and his tender mercies are over all his works.*

10 *All thy works shall praise thee, O Lord; and thy saints shall bless thee.*

11 *They shall speak of the glory of thy kingdom, and talk of thy power;*

12 *To make known to the sons of men his mighty acts, and the glorious majesty of his kingdom.*

13   *Thy kingdom is an everlasting kingdom, and thy dominion endureth throughout all generations.*

14   *The LORD upholdeth all that fall, and raiseth up all those that be bowed down.*

15   *The eyes of all wait upon thee; and thou givest them their meat in due season.*

16   *Thou openest thine hand, and satisfiest the desire of every living thing.*

17   *The LORD is righteous in all his ways, and holy in all his works.*

18   *The LORD is nigh unto all them that call upon him, to all that call upon him in truth.*

19   *He will fulfil the desire of them that fear him: he also will hear their cry, and will save them.*

20   *The LORD preserveth all them that love him: but all the wicked will he destroy.*

21   *My mouth shall speak the praise of the LORD: and let all flesh bless his holy name for ever and ever.*

Psalm 145

I always disliked it when other people, especially rich people, say that there is no happiness in possessions. Now, I too, must be added to the list. I have many wonderful things. I like a powerful and high-quality car. My home is beautiful with many exceptional amenities. But they do not make me happy or sad. They just are.

My happiness has different roots, and the older I get the more important these become. I've found I'm happy when I'm with others. I'm happy when my wife and I are together. I'm happy in the scriptures. I'm happy giving service—money, time, or things. I'm happiest of all when I'm closest to God.

Allow me to suggest 11 ways to bring more happiness into our lives. There is no particular order, and I'm sure many reading this book are well ahead of me on most of these things.

1. Stay Close To God.

Be happy while you take this very seriously.

> [8] *This book of the law shall not depart out of thy mouth; but thou shalt meditate therein day and night, that thou mayest observe to do according to all that is written therein: for then thou shalt make thy way prosperous, and then thou shalt have good success.*
>
> *Joshua 1:8*

Study this book. Find time to think and ponder. Pray often. Make prayer an important daily activity.

2. Keep Your Life Simple.

"Avoid costly entanglements." —George Washington.

Avoid confusing relationships. Spend time enjoying the simple things of life. Spend more time with your kids. Spend more and better time with your parents. Spend more time with animals.

3. Be Cheerful With Others.

Uplift, edify, and bring out the good in others. Be a *true* friend. Never, never speak ill of anyone. Avoid rumors, put a stop to them. Don't get caught up in gossip and nay-saying.

Smile at everyone, and express pleasant salutations. Inquire honestly about others. Make your greetings and departings sweet.

> [47] *And if ye salute your brethren only, what do ye more than others? do not even the publicans so?*
>
> *Matthew 5:47*

4. Keep Studying.

Become an eternal student. Read. Stay a step ahead by knowing what your education will do for you, but don't limit yourself. Take *worthwhile* classes. Read the *best* books, and acquire and use a good reference library. Learning new and important things is a fulfilling activity in and of itself.

5. Treat Each Day Special.

Be happy in the day. Each day has a treasure waiting. Our attitude will help us see things in their proper light. Observe nature. Our innovative nature and aptitude for change and understanding will help as we greet, meet, and complete each day.

6. Develop Grace.

27 *...for I am gracious.*

Exodus 22:27

A truly caring and giving attitude goes a long way. Murphy is everywhere, and many around us have problems. A gracious and graceful demeanor will add depth and beauty to your life and the lives of others. Life's unpleasant moments need us to step up and rise above each negative occasion.

8 *The LORD is gracious, and full of compassion; slow to anger, and of great mercy.*

Psalm 145:8

7. Live A Life Of Serendipity.

Serendipity is a happy or joyous discovery found while looking for something else. New friends, procedures, products, and services await. Don't be close-minded. Observe. Pray for new discoveries. Live a serendipitous life.

8. Think Big.

The world is full of small stuff—minutia. Most of it gets in the way. If you want great results, think of great ways to accomplish them. Rise above the ordinary. Stick out. Every day do exceptional things. Dazzle yourself.

Be definite. Let your yes be yes and your no be no. However, don't make mountains out of molehills. Thinking big is worthy of the effort, but others will drag you down. Help them see the big picture. Stay on track.

9. Think Noble.

What good can come from small or petty thinking? Let your actions follow wise and noble thoughts. Lift, inspire, and be not ordinary.

We are children of God. We owe Him no less than to act as His offspring. He desires us to be joint-heirs; then act this way. Our careers, our businesses, and our relationships should move in the direction of wonderful and noble pursuits.

Life is too short for the petty, small, and unimportant things. Start today cleaning out those harmful characteristics and demeaning ways. Substitute them for truth, good things, and good living. Watch your happiness grow as your days are spent this ennobling way.

10.   Build Others.

Don't be a stumbling block. Help others conceptualize block-busting so they can move forward. Everyone's life is full of doubt and uncertainty. Life has many dark moments. Be a light.

> 14   *Ye are the light of the world. A city that is set on an hill cannot be hid.*
>
> 15   *Neither do men light a candle, and put it under a bushel, but on a candlestick; and it giveth light unto all that are in the house.*
>
> 16   *Let your light so shine before men, that they may see your good works, and glorify your Father which is in heaven.*
>
> *Matthew 5:14-16*

If you don't know how to be a light, then use the gospel for a track to run on. God is very concerned how we treat each other. He said, "By this shall all men know that ye are my disciples, if ye have love one to another." (John 13:35) If you need His help, ask for it.

> 7 *Ask, and it shall be given you; seek, and ye shall find; knock, and it shall be opened unto you:*
>
> 8 *For every one that asketh receiveth; and he that seeketh findeth; and to him that knocketh it shall be opened.*
>
> 9 *Or what man is there of you, whom if his son ask bread, will he give him a stone?*
>
> 10 *Or if he ask a fish, will he give him a serpent?*
>
> 11 *If ye then, being evil, know how to give good gifts unto your children, how much more shall your Father which is in heaven give good things to them that ask him?*
>
> 12 *Therefore all things whatsoever ye would that men should do to you, do ye even so to them: for this is the law and the prophets.*
>
> *Matthew 7:7-12*

Strengthen, build—don't judge and don't begrudge. Be honestly happy for others. If someone succeeds at a task, praise and celebrate with them. Don't make people wonder what you're thinking. To me, any excuse is good for a party or a get-together. You can't build and uplift people unless you're with them. (A letter, a phone call or a fax is okay though.) If you're going to make excuses to have a party, why not celebrate the everyday things, such as a birthday, winning a horse class, a good report card, or just because "it's Tuesday."

We are all like giant ships moving through life. A small tugboat only moves us a little, but it gets our course straight, or helps us get to where we need to be. Be a tugboat for others.

11. Quit Making Excuses.

We, as Americans, are great at making excuses. Some have elevated it to a high form of art. However, it's detrimental.

Apologize and get on. Don't get caught up in this cycle of losing. It's a poor part of our attitude and needs to be eliminated.

Can you see God making excuses? Can you see Jesus making excuses while He is hanging on the cross? He did not. About others, he just forgave them. They didn't know what they were doing.

Recently, I was sharing with my family the poignant story of the Good Samaritan. The Jew, by the roadside, was beaten and robbed. The man from Samaria took care of him, and agreed to return and pay more if necessary.

It's a great story, and more powerful when you realize it's for us. Jesus was answering a question about loving our neighbor. It seems someone wanted an excuse to only love whom he wanted to love. "Who is my neighbor?" Jesus asked. I love this story. However, it reminds me that I have a long way to go.

I heard a modern day take on this parable. A wise man asked if I had time for a little levity. I said, "Yes." He told me that two liberals passed by the bloodied, beaten up man, and one said to the other, "The person who did this to that man needs help."

Excuses are demeaning. Avoid them. Be of good cheer.

The list could go on. There are so many wonderful characteristics and personal traits we need to develop. Every day brings new opportunities for growth. Work on one at a time if you need to, but do so every day. Your journey of a thousand miles must start today.

I started this chapter by writing about wanting to be happy. I'll reiterate the same here. You have to want to be happy. Oh, we all need to be this way, but it is the wanting that propels us. We don't need to be happy all the time. There is a time for sorrow. Jesus wept. He cried over Jerusalem. Other great players on the stage of life have had travails and bad experiences. Many have had to overcome severe hardships.

There may not have been many happy times. However, it's the trials that shape and make who we are, no matter what they are. Suffering makes us better—more tolerant, able to cope, hopeful, patient, and wise or bitter—negative, demeaning, impatient, and sad. You choose: better or bitter.

Again, everyday we have opportunities to raise our flag and show our colors. So, even though there is a place and time for sorrow, our strivings should be for the pursuit of excellent happiness.

9

Father, forgive me my injuries,
as I forgive those I have injured!
—Robert Traill Spence Lowell

Forgiveness

Let me tell a story to illustrate a good starting point for this chapter. First though, if you don't believe in right and wrong, if you don't believe in a merciful, yet just God, then not much I'm going to write will be meaningful. These concepts are firmly based in the Bible and have far-reaching "everyday" consequences. I'm going to conclude with this: that to be really happy we must forgive others (for infractions big and small) every day. Please don't get turned off by that, maybe thinking you have no one to forgive. Stick with me and I hope this will make sense to you.

Lake Tahoe

Every few months our company sponsors a really great event, the Executive Retreat in Lake Tahoe, Nevada. I want to make several small points along the way, so indulge me as I tell you briefly about this event. A big part of our company's mission is to teach people how to build, enhance, and protect their assets better. As a matter of fact, let me list our company's mission statement:

1. Help people make more money in business, real estate, and the stock market.

2. Help people seriously reduce exposure to risk and liability.

3. Help businesses and people reduce their tax liability.

4. Help prepare people for a great retirement.

5. Make sure people's families or churches are bequeathed all possessions in a "TLC" way.

6. Conduct our business using Biblical standards.

Part of this process is teaching people about Pension Plans, Living Trusts, Charitable Reminder Trusts, Nevada Corporations, et cetera. I don't think any other company in America comes close to our great seminars and workbooks.

Many years ago, a dilemma developed. We were so good at educating people that they wanted us to set up or establish their Nevada Corporations, Pension Plans, and all the rest.

At first, we contracted with Nevada Corporation Companies, but received such poor service that it led us to open our own office there. We also have internal processing people and a dedicated staff who set up all these entities. We have set up thousands of Nevada Corporations.

Another problem was helping people to understand and use Nevada Corporations properly. We decided to have a giant board of directors meeting and have everyone bring their documents to one place so they could all learn how to be effective at running their corporations. It's a great event; it's the most fun of all our events.

I do a one-and-a-half hour presentation on getting rich in America. At our last board of directors meeting, I felt something should be added to my talk. It was a strong feeling, one that I've not had before in regard to my speaking.

I was talking about building a family dynasty, using kids, grandparents, et cetera to build the family business. Then, out of the blue, I started talking about forgiving. My mouth was saying words I had not thought of before. I paused.

I looked out into the audience through very bright lights (it was a big high stage). I was able to see bodies, but was not able to look into their eyes. I said, "Someone must need this information." I only said a paragraph or two, and it could be summarized like this: "We need to forgive each other. Families are split up for the most trivial of reasons. An unkind word, a petty argument, or a complete misunderstanding may have a family torn apart for years. The original offense can barely be remembered, but it's time to go home and say, 'I'm sorry' or 'Please forgive me.'"

I said other things, but I think you get the point. I strongly felt that the small pain or inconvenience of saying and believing the words "I'm sorry" would far surpass the pain of continued bitterness of having families divided or not remaining as strong and cohesive as they could and should be.

I realize I could say that same speech today to any group of even 12 people and someone would be touched. The response that night was quite overwhelming. Many waited until the crowds died down, and more spoke to me the next day. Their responses, however, were basically the same: "were you talking to me?" or "I'm going to call my brother, we haven't talked for 18 years." This happened over a dozen times.

Only twice was there time and privacy enough for me to ask what happened to cause the problem. Both times the response was the same: "Oh, it's so petty." "It's so stupid." They remembered the gist of the problem, but both said it was blown way out of proportion.

We seem so quick to find fault, so rash in our judgment. We then build mountains out of molehills. And mountains are hard to climb, let alone tear down. Look at the following scripture:

> 5 *For thou, LORD, art good, and ready to forgive; and plenteous in mercy unto all them that call upon thee.*
>
> *Psalm 86:5*

I love the expression "plenteous in mercy." It has so much meaning. God is capable of seeing us, and He will have mercy to balance the demand for justice. Isn't that what the Savior came for—to bring us back to God? If He is willing to forgive us, how much more so should we be willing to forgive others? If this seems tough, you may not want to read on. Remember, I'm using this as a base to get to a more significant way of life.

Casting Stones

One of my favorite stories of the New Testament is one where the woman caught in the act of adultery is brought before Jesus. It's found in the book of John. I love Jesus' response and also how He did it. He knelt down. He slowed everything down. By the old law, they had every right to stone her. I think he knew that very few righteous people were left after so many years of perverting the laws. He wrote in the sand. He then questioned, even challenged—"He that is without sin among you, let him first cast a stone at her." (John 8:7) What an incredible piece of advice! What wisdom! How can we have such behavior? In other places, we're told "Judge not, that ye be not judged." (Matthew 7:1) Build on this. If we're not to exercise unrighteous judgment (we are called upon to make judgment calls daily) then how can we be so prideful as to condemn others?

The part I like the best is this: Jesus could have judged her. He was the only one who could have. He could have condemned her by the law. He could have thrown the book at her; but then, the crowd dispersed, and he gave her the finale of all final responses:

> 10 *When Jesus had lifted up himself, and saw none but the woman, he said unto her, Woman, where are those thine accusers? hath no man condemned thee?*
>
> 11 *She said, No man, LORD. And Jesus said unto her, Neither do I condemn thee: go, and sin no more.*
>
> *John 8:10-11*

This story is so important to me because I have hoped that it will be the same with me.

> ⁷ *Remember not the sins of my youth, nor my trans-gressions: according to thy mercy remember thou me for thy goodness' sake, O LORD.*
>
> *Psalm 25:7*

Look at the type of action God takes if we repent, or walk uprightly and sin no more. Look at these. I could have listed more.

> ⁷ *Keeping mercy for thousands, forgiving iniquity and transgression and sin.*
>
> *Exodus 34:7*

> ¹⁸ *The LORD is longsuffering and of great mercy, for-giving iniquity and transgression, and by no means clearing the guilty.*
>
> *Numbers 14:18*

It's obvious God calls people out of sin and then to re-pentance and "sinning no more," and then forgiveness oc-curs.

> ¹⁸ *Come now, and let us reason together, saith the LORD: though your sins be as scarlet, they shall be as white as snow; though they be red like crimson, they shall be as wool.*
>
> *Isaiah 1:18*

> ⁷ *And he laid it upon my mouth, and said, Lo, this hath touched thy lips; and thine iniquity is taken away, and thy sin purged.*
>
> *Isaiah 6:7*

> ²⁰ *In those days, and in that time, saith the LORD, the iniquity of Israel shall be sought for, and there shall*

> *be none; and the sins of Judah, and they shall not be found: for I will pardon them whom I reserve.*

> *Jeremiah 50:20*

> ¹⁸ *Who is a GOD like unto thee, that pardoneth iniquity, and passeth by the transgression of the remnant of his heritage? he retaineth not his anger for ever, because he delighteth in mercy.*

> *Micah 7:18*

> ¹⁶ *None of his sins that he hath committed shall be mentioned unto him: he hath done that which is lawful and right; he shall surely live.*

> *Ezekiel 33:16*

Okay, now we know what God has done and what He will do. Isn't it comforting to have these assurances?

Let's move on and see how we are to act. Paul gives us a gentle admonition—but it's of a dynamism that cannot be denied:

> ³² *And be ye kind one to another, tenderhearted, forgiving one another, even as GOD for Christ's sake hath forgiven you.*

> *Ephesians 4:32*

In Matthew 18, we have a specific challenge:

> ¹⁵ *Moreover if thy brother shall trespass against thee, go and tell him his fault between thee and him alone: if he shall hear thee, thou hast gained thy brother.*

> *Matthew 18:15*

The challenge is more direct in Luke:

> ³ *Take heed to yourselves: if thy brother trespass against thee, rebuke him; and if he repent, forgive him.*

> *Luke 17:3*

The plot thickens as the offense continues:

⁴ *And if he trespasses against thee seven times in a
day, and seven times in a day turn again to thee,
saying, I repent; thou shalt forgive him.*

Luke 17:4

Read the response in verse five.

⁵ *And the apostles said unto the LORD, Increase our
faith.*

Luke 17:5

I love that line. Of course it's tough, and you and I will
find it difficult; but there must be a reason for His statement.
Could it be that we will have to be forgiven by Him this
many times or more?

And if any of us should get caught up thinking we are
better than anyone else and if we think they should kowtow
to us, read the following parable:

¹ *And Jesus entered and passed through Jericho.*

² *And, behold, there was a man named Zacchaeus,
which was the chief among the publicans, and he
was rich.*

³ *And he sought to see Jesus who he was; and could
not for the press, because he was little of stature.*

⁴ *And he ran before, and climbed up into a sycamore
tree to see him: for he was to pass that way.*

⁵ *And when Jesus came to the place, he looked up,
and saw him, and said unto him, Zacchaeus, make
haste, and come down; for today I must abide at
thy house.*

⁶ *And he made haste, and came down, and received
him joyfully.*

⁷ *And when they saw it, they all murmured, saying,
That he was gone to be guest with a man that is a
sinner.*

⁸ *And Zacchaeus stood, and said unto the* LORD*; Behold,* LORD*, the half of my goods I give to the poor; and if I have taken any thing from any man by false accusation, I restore him fourfold.*

⁹ *And Jesus said unto him, This day is salvation come to this house, forsomuch as he also is a son of Abraham.*

Luke 19:1-9

(Remember a publican was a tax collector and despised by many.) Many did not understand why Jesus would associate with such a person. They were better, they thought. They reasoned that Jesus should be with them. Jesus' response in verse ten is quite instructive.

¹⁰ *For the Son of man is come to seek and to save that which was lost.*

Luke 19:10

We all fall short of the glory of God, but He will take care of us. Look at these words from Hebrews:

¹² *For I will be merciful to their unrighteous, and their sins and their iniquities will I remember no more."*

Hebrews 8:12

It's clear He wants us to forgive others. And with this next scripture we get closer to my main point.

³⁷ *Judge not, and ye shall not be judged: condemn not, and ye shall not be condemned: forgive, and ye shall be forgiven:*

Luke 6:37

An awesome lesson in love, life, and learning. I cannot add more to this verse. Please read it again. Divide up each part. Spend time with it. Ponder it. Think of its ramifications. Think of life with and without this verse. It's just simply powerful.

God loves us, this I'm sure. He gives us commandments because of His love. He chastens us because of His love. He wants us to come back to Him and even sacrificed His beloved Son to make that possible for us.

> 23 *Have I any pleasure at all that the wicked should die? saith the* LORD GOD: *and not that he should return from his ways, and live?*
>
> Ezekiel 18:23

Everything then must make sense. Why is He so into helping us with our relationships? Why does He want us to love one another?

> 34 *A new commandment I give unto you, That ye love one another; as I have loved you, that ye also love one another.*
>
> John 13:34

Why does he want us to be united and be one with each other?

> 20 *Neither pray I for these alone, but for them also which shall believe on me through their word;*
> 21 *That they all may be one; as thou, Father, art in me, and I in thee, that they also may be one in us: that the world may believe that thou hast sent me.*
> 22 *And the glory which thou gavest me I have given them; that they may be one, even as we are one:*
> 23 *I in them, and thou in me, that they may be made perfect in one; and that the world may know that thou hast sent me, and hast loved them, as thou hast loved me.*
>
> John 17:20-23

Answer these questions and you uncover a wonderful lesson, and then carry on. How can we be and do these things if we have bad feelings, hate others, or have animosity toward anyone? We can't!

The commandment to forgive others is a commandment of happiness. It is, in its basic sense, a cleansing process. It purges us and makes us receptacles for God's spirit and love.

What would a life be like without forgiveness? I think we see it in people who hold grudges. They don't forgive, nor forget. They are not happy people. It's as if the sun does not rise in their lives.

However, look at others who are full of love and willing to quickly forgive. That's important; forgive quickly. Don't let it fester. Don't surround yourself with negative feelings. They hurt, they destroy, and quite frankly, they serve no purpose whatsoever.

Forgiving and forgetting is a wonderful formula for success. Read once again a portion of the Lord's Prayer.

> 12   *And forgive us our debts, as we forgive our debtors.*

> *Matthew 6:12*

> *Actions are ours; their consequences belong to heaven.*
> *—Sir Philip Francis*

The Miracle of Forgiving

This section is not about miracles. A brief discussion of miracles, however, is in order so that a major point may be made and understood later on.

To me, a miracle is an unexplainable event. It is an act of God. Miracles are done for a purpose. They are usually simple, yet very meaningful to the participants. Whether a miracle is accomplished by a direct divine intervention and a change of substance, events, or responses; or whether it is the use of natural laws and phenomenon, it matters not to me. Both are miracles.

Miracles help God's purposes. In His divine economy, nothing is wasted. If we are in tune to His spiritual thoughts, we will experience miracles constantly. We can even bring them about by prayer, by obeying the commandments, and being in the covenant. Think of it. If God is to bless us as we become a covenant person, then these "inexplicable" blessings are miracles. There is no explanation (at least to the rational human mind) for the occurrence.

I'm amazed that people try to minimize God's wonderful hand and handiwork in the lives of His children. They try to explain away all of His wonders. They think that by explaining the miracles in rational, "worldly," and politically correct ways, it will help. It doesn't. It takes us farther from Him.

Let me give an example: Sodom and Gomorrah. Those two cities burned up. God was explicit in his demands—His reward and punishment. They flunked the test and "bam," they were gone. Now some try to rationalize, to minimize, and to disprove God's action. They say there were natural oil pockets—fire bogs—under the end of the lake. These skeptics believe that this area of fossil fuel caught on fire, and the cities were in the way.

So what? What if the recent findings are true? If God created the universe, this world, and the north end of the lake this way, why can't he use natural resources and natural processes to accomplish His Word? It's still a magnificent event—by any standards.

One of my points is that God wants to be remembered. He told us He's a jealous God. He wants our devotion and He wants it in an endearing and enduring manner. When He comes into our lives, He leaves tracks. He leaves things for us to remember Him by.

One such "track" occurred in my life. I share it here for a few reasons. One is to prove this last point by using a meaningful story out of my own life. The other reason I'll explain at the end of the story.

When I was about 28 years old, I was heavily involved in buying and selling real estate. I was building a fortune—

very involved and very busy. I had been a cab driver before and developed a tendency to drive fast.

One day I was heading for the office. I took a shortcut after exiting the freeway, went around a hill, and headed toward a very busy street. The light was green. My office was one block on the other side of this street. I timed the lights and would cruise through this busy intersection at about 25 to 30 miles per hour. The corner had three to four-story buildings on all four sides. I couldn't see either direction as I approached this street until I was right up to the crosswalk.

Usually, when approaching this corner, I slowed down to 25 or so. This morning I was the only car on my approach. I passed the alley (halfway) and distinctly heard a voice in my mind say, "SLOW DOWN." It was so real. I immediately hit the brakes. I was down to under five miles per hour, almost to a stop by the time I was at the crosswalk. Remember, I had the green light.

I looked to my left instantaneously and an old beat up station wagon sped through the red light at 60 to 70 miles per hour. There is no doubt in my mind that I would have been hit on my side—probably at the door.

I'll never forget that day. It still gives me chills when I think of it. I go to Tacoma often and frequently visit that block, because one of my favorite Chinese restaurants is a few doors away.

I guess it wasn't my time to go; I have too many imperfections that I need to work on. There is no way you can tell me there is not divine intervention in the affairs of men and women. Miracles are everywhere.

This leads to the second reason why I tell this story. This explanation will hopefully make more sense as I get to the main theme of this chapter. Here it is: many people who have read this story, or many people who hear such stories, just sluff them off. They're embarrassed by them. Maybe such experiences make them feel uncomfortable.

I hope you're not one of them. I think that if you're still reading, then shared experiences like these are interesting, faith promoting, and possibly spiritual. I pray also that they give us hope. Believe me, if God helps one as bad as I was, then He'll help people far superior in spirituality than me. As a matter of fact, His hand is extended to all.

I love receiving mailed-in stories about God's miracles. Marriages, seemingly on the rocks, saved and rebuilt strong. Family ties strengthen. Friendships knit together. People turn to God. People strengthen their resolve to change, to repent, to live better lives. Miracles are all around.

Do You Want More Miracles?

If you like the last part, then read on. I have found one surefire way to seek and have God's help in any life. Sometimes the help is manifest as gentle feelings and inspiration and sometimes as "inexplicable" miracles.

This idea stems from the greatest miracle of all: salvation. I know this is heavy duty but stick with me on this. God loves us. He wants us to come back to Him. He even gave us a Messiah, a Savior.

He wants to bless us way beyond our ability to comprehend. It is definitely beyond what I deserve. My good friend Steve Bird, author of *Prayers That Bring Miracles*, shared with me an interesting perspective. He said, "We do all we can, we repent, try, fail, and try again. When it's all done, we still do not measure up, but a plan of redemption is prepared for us. Our redeemer makes up the difference. He fills in the gap."

What a comfort! What hope! And now listen to what He asks in return: He wants our hearts in the right place. Furthermore, He is willing to forgive us—even to the extent of paying for our sins. This is a full redemption. Read Psalm 130:7.

7   *Let Israel hope in the L*ORD*: for with the L*ORD *there*
     is mercy, and with him is plenteous redemption.

Wow! Plenteous redemption. I need it. This act of forgiveness is so wonderful, so all encompassing, that it gives
pause for thought.

Should we follow this example? Should His words on
this matter be followed? Paul told us to work out our own
salvation with fear and trembling. The question is simple:
should we forgive? Should we forgive completely and unconditionally? Well, the scriptures tell us to. They even say
to forgive our enemies. My goodness, it's tough enough to
forgive those we love let alone our enemies. The Bible goes
on and says to pray for them that despitefully use us. Man,
this gets tough.

This discussion could get really heavy, but that's not my
intention. My purpose here is to give a clear, functional, and
helpful approach to a process that each of us needs to get on
and stay on. I'm not here to convert anyone but to share a
few scriptures and thoughts that have worked for me. This
method gives a way to bring miracles into your life.

It's simple: forgive others. Forgive them often, forgive
them completely, and if possible, forget about it.

A Cleansing Process

In an all-encompassing way, forgiving opens us to the
spiritual side of life. It starts the process of cleaning up our
own lives. We must check the beam in our own eye and
forgive the speck in our brother's.

Forgiveness is an act of giving. It becomes easy to give
money, other possessions, and even time. A life of forgiving
is a great life indeed:

31   *Let all bitterness, and wrath, and anger, and*
     clamour, and evil speaking, be put away from you,
     with all malice:

> ³² *And be ye kind one to another, tenderhearted, for-*
> *giving one another, even as G*OD *for Christ's sake*
> *hath forgiven you.*
>
> *Ephesians 4:31, 32*

A life of forgiving adds another dimension. Forgiving is powerful. It might be painful, it might require swallowing a lot of pride, it might seem impossible, but rest assured, whatever the price, it's worth it!

Let's Get Started

As always, the place to start is with our own family. Again, God has set the example. He has made it possible for the whole human race to be forgiven. It is His wonderful gift. It is the gift of all gifts. Specifically, He had a chosen people, a covenant people. As I wrote in *Business Buy The Bible*, Christ fulfilled this covenant and gave us a new covenant, one with better promises. Most specifically, He has given each of us, individually, a way to be forgiven and come back to him.

Now, He asks us to not judge, but to love, to be kind, to have charity, and to forgive. I'm sure the family is a great place to practice this forgiving process. In close quarters, with sibling competition, with parents' desires at odds with their children's desires, bad things are said and done.

Start here, forgive them. Don't try to change the other person. That is not part of the process. Don't forgive with conditions or preconceived expectations. Don't worry about the other person's reaction. It will be what it will be. Don't let their reaction, lack of attention, or unresponsiveness offend you or alter your course. It is not your job to always make it right.

Just forgive them unconditionally. This is your cleansing process, not theirs.

And don't, don't, don't be judgmental or condescending. If you have wronged someone, or feel that they have wronged you, look at this wise comment:

23 *Therefore if thou bring thy gift to the altar, and there rememberest that thy brother hath ought against thee;*

24 *Leave there thy gift before the altar, and go thy way; first be reconciled to thy brother, and then come and offer thy gift.*

Matthew 5:23, 24

Follow this simple procedure. If appropriate, read this scripture together.

I've had several times when forgiveness was needed. Relations were strained. Yes, sometimes time heals wounds, but far too often wounds never heal. They get worse. The pride, bad memories, and anger continue, and the cycle must be broken. Often, people can't even remember the original problem. The words said in the pursuing years, the bad feelings, the sarcasm, and innuendo all have taken center stage. Battle lines have been drawn, family and friends recruited.

It's time to end the cycle. The conflict, especially between family members, has to stop. Why? Because wonderful blessings are stopped or slowed down. A wonderful relationship with help, admiration, support, and love ends. Look at the cost; it's just too high. The fear, embarrassment, and humility needed for a humble apology, or seeking forgiveness, is a small price to pay for the peaceful and joyful result that comes as a consequence of this forgiving.

If all you can do is forgive silently, let it start there. Develop good feelings. It is infinitely better, in most instances, to do so face-to-face, verbally. Have patience for the results. Don't judge. Again, it is you that is to do what God said. If good is to happen, it will happen.

Friends

Now on to friends, co-workers, bosses, employees, and all others: in everyday commerce and relationships, a happy yet contemplative, humble yet confident, attitude is to be prized. If you are over two years old, you've stepped on a lot of toes, and you've probably spoken rumors or negative words. The list could go on. Now, get on with life.

Everyday forgive someone, even yourself. God loves you; what then makes you think less of yourself?

23 *Therefore is the kingdom of heaven likened unto a certain king, which would take account of his servants.*

24 *And when he had begun to reckon, one was brought unto him, which owed him ten thousand talents.*

25 *But forasmuch as he had not to pay, his lord commanded him to be sold, and his wife, and children, and all that he had, and payment to be made.*

26 *The servant therefore fell down, and worshipped him, saying, Lord, have patience with me, and I will pay thee all.*

27 *Then the lord of that servant was moved with compassion, and loosed him, and forgave him the debt.*

28 *But the same servant went out, and found one of his fellowservants, which owed him an hundred pence: and he laid hands on him, and took him by the throat, saying, Pay me that thou owest.*

29 *And his fellowservant fell down at his feet, and besought him, saying, Have patience with me, and I will pay thee all.*

30 *And he would not: but went and cast him into prison, till he should pay the debt.*

31 *So when his fellowservants saw what was done, they were very sorry, and came and told unto their lord all that was done.*

32 *Then his lord, after that he had called him, said unto him, O thou wicked servant, I forgave thee all that debt, because thou desiredst me:*

33 *Shouldest not thou also have had compassion on thy fellowservant, even as I had pity on thee?*

34 *And his lord was wroth, and delivered him to the tormentors, till he should pay all that was due unto him.*

35 *So likewise shall my heavenly Father do also unto you, if ye from your hearts forgive not every one his brother their trespasses.*

Matthew 18:23-35

There is another by-product to forgiving friends. It's catchy. It spreads like wildfire. More and better work gets done. Our minds are freed up to be creative and do more good. Forgiveness is a solid building block to add to building relationships.

Enemies

The scriptures are explicit. From the Old Testament we read about loving our neighbor. Often the people were told to treat each other with kindness. The hardest thing in that era was to take in strangers and treat them as "one born among you."

The people were constantly reminded in these discourses of their captivity in Egypt. They were strangers there. At times it was really bad for them. How could they be expected to kindly treat people with pent-up hostility, clinging to bad memories? They found it difficult. They had to forgive first. These are great stories from which we can gain strength.

The New Testament has an array of poignant and helpful scriptures, the foremost being to turn the other cheek:

38 *Ye have heard that it hath been said, An eye for an eye, and a tooth for a tooth:*

39 *But I say unto you, That ye resist not evil: but whosoever shall smite thee on thy right cheek, turn to him the other also.*

40 *And if any man will sue thee at the law, and take away thy coat, let him have thy cloak also.*

41   *And whosoever shall compel thee to go a mile, go with him twain.*

42   *Give to him that asketh thee, and from him that would borrow of thee turn not thou away.*

43   *Ye have heard that it hath been said, Thou shalt love thy neighbour, and hate thine enemy.*

44   *But I say unto you, Love your enemies, bless them that curse you, do good to them that hate you, and pray for them which despitefully use you, and persecute you;*

Matthew 5:38-44

These are wonderful commandments. Let's learn them, love them, and live them.

Along with the cleansing process, and the wonderful freedom that forgiving people gives us, there is another by-product. Forgiving puts us in a framework to make our lives better. It lets us glimpse at the other side of the human relationship with God.

If we want to improve, we must repent. We must change and grow. A wise man, when asked, "Who is righteous?" answered, "one who is repenting." This is what God asked. Then the circle is complete. If God is willing to forgive, and if we follow His commands, love Him, and repent, then all will be well.

This process can start today for all of us by simply forgiving and then perfecting this humbling good work. We then will see miracles all around us. He forgave us; can we do no less to others?

10

If thou hast abundance, give alms accordingly: if thou have but a little, be not afraid to give according to that little.
—The Apocrypha, Tobit 4:8

Sharing Abundance

My business has been good, and many are doing well. They have good jobs and fulfilling careers, are buying homes, et cetera. The more I receive the more I want to share. The actions are not something I've made up or have to work hard to do. The older I get, the more I read, the more I learn and apply the scriptures, the more I want to do what the scriptures say.

It is difficult writing this without sounding like I'm bragging. I just want to be good in the lives of others.

The money, the wealth, is beyond anything I deserve. Therefore, I treat it like a steward. What am I doing with it? What good can it be used for? Is the gaining of these extra talents noble, good, and honest?

Sharing is not just something I do; it has become something I am. I hope you have experiences that lead you to this point just as I have been led. God is kind, and He has been very patient. I'm far from being done. I pray to stay on the right road.

I want people around me to come along. When I discover a new stock market technique, I try it, test it, and then share it with others. I keep producing tapes and books to help others. Yes, we make money at our business, but we get nothing out of what people do; we sell books and seminars; they keep the profits.

Hopefully in this process we've shared a few insights that are brought about by our application of scriptural truths. People now ask me why we use the scriptures so much. It's simple. They are worthy to share. Sadly, many have turned from them. Throughout history and even in the founding of our country, they were part of our discourse—often the whole discourse. Have you noticed that we, as a nation—even the political leaders—are turning from this great book, the Bible? Why? Would we rather listen to political friends, men, than God? Alas, I think it has come to that.

I want to bring the Bible back into business talks, and into government debate and action. Government cannot impose its way on religion, but surely religion can impose its way on government. Our founding fathers knew this and used the truths of the Bible to build great characters. These great characters then built this country. Turn from this method and we turn to our peril. I love to share these truths. People don't need these truths pounded into their heads; they quietly nod their heads as they recognize eternal truths. God's words are eternal.

My life is so full; I have more than enough; I want others to join in. Carl, a good friend, approached me one evening and told me there was a scripture he'd like to share with me. This evening's affairs were quite busy, but I took time right then to go to a quiet part of the room and he shared his thoughts with me.

He started reading from Luke, chapter five. I'll list all the verses here and then tell you what I remember of his thoughts. Carl had attended one year of seminary to prepare for the ministry. He knew these verses well.

1   *And it came to pass, that, as the people pressed upon him to hear the word of GOD, he stood by the lake of Gennesaret,*

2   *And saw two ships standing by the lake: but the fishermen were gone out of them, and were washing their nets.*

3   *And he entered into one of the ships, which was Simon's, and prayed him that he would thrust out a little from the land. And he sat down, and taught the people out of the ship.*

4   *Now when he had left speaking, he said unto Simon, Launch out into the deep, and let down your nets for a draught.*

5   *And Simon answering said unto him, Master, we have toiled all the night, and have taken nothing: nevertheless at thy word I will let down the net.*

6   *And when they had this done, they enclosed a great multitude of fishes: and their net brake.*

7   *And they beckoned unto their partners, which were in the other ship, that they should come and help them. And they came, and filled both the ships, so that they began to sink.*

8   *When Simon Peter saw it, he fell down at Jesus' knees, saying, Depart from me; for I am a sinful man, O Lord.*

9   *For he was astonished, and all that were with him, at the draught of the fishes which they had taken:*

10   *And so was also James, and John, the sons of Zebedee, which were partners with Simon. And Jesus said unto Simon, Fear not; from henceforth thou shalt catch men.*

11   *And when they had brought their ships to land, they forsook all, and followed him.*

Luke 5:1-11

Carl pointed out to me that "Ships are safe in the harbor, but that's not what ships are for," and that you can't catch big fish in shallow waters. I'm not a fisherman, but I don't think you can catch large quantities of fish in shallow water either. But most importantly, God can't bless you if you don't do what He says.

This is how I feel. My life is so full. I know many people far more spiritual than I. I am a babe in the woods when it comes to spiritual things. It must not matter the age, the status, or the accomplishments of one whom God blesses. When the nets are breaking, it's time to share. Look, they called for help and all who participated were blessed.

Obviously, the fish here represent the word of God. Peter received much. He wanted to share. Look at the end of verse 10:

> [10] *Fear not; from henceforth thou shalt catch men.*
> *And when they had brought their ships to land,*
> *they forsook all, and followed him.*
>
> *Luke 5:10*

Back to the verses in Luke. I appreciate Carl's showing me additional meaning in these verses. I've read them before, as have many of you, but this night I gained an added understanding. I do believe in serendipity. There are other messages to be found, other wisdom to gain. This reading was special because these verses took on added meaning. It was a wonderful way to end the evening. I went to sleep thinking of Peter and the bulging nets.

And, think of this. These fishermen probably just had the best day of fishing in their lives. Their boats were full. The whole village could eat and be full. They could eat their fill, then pickle, dry, season with salt for storage, and other things that sea villages do with fish. Surely such an abundance of fish could be used for trading and acquiring many other useful things. It was a great day. It was memorable.

And then, upon their boats landing, they simply gave it all up and followed Jesus. Does this not help us put the things in our lives in proper order? This could have been the beginning of a great fishing business, but there was more important work to do. God used these experiences to point the way to better things so they would have meaningful miracles deeply embedded in their memories and in their lives.

My humble prayer is that we come to an understanding of how great God our Father is and dedicate our lives to serving Him by serving others.

11

Keep On Track

I hope one of the hallmarks of my seminars has been the giving of useful, functional, even doable information. The results sure bespeak that end. There is a process to my method: 1.) Teach information that will change lives and literally modify people's behavior. Don't just teach information for information's sake. 2.) Teach only achievable things, things people can do. Yes, stretch people a little, but let them be able to accomplish the task. 3.) Make sure the change or action is reportable, and the result or target is clear and definable. Progress, once accomplished, can proceed. There's nothing like progress proceeding.

I've used this process in Sunday school, in real estate seminars, in leadership training events—virtually everywhere. I don't just teach it; I live it. Let me share with you some additional methods I use to be "big time" successful.

1. Do things that can be duplicated. Duplication and repetition are the keys to success.

2. Think big in a whole bunch of bite-size pieces. McDonalds doesn't make all of its money each year selling one big gigantic hamburger. They sell billions of little ones.

3. Make money, not excuses. Life is too short to spend any time at all with depressing negative statements. There is a trade-off: you get paid for what you do. Show me one dollar you've made from making excuses.

4. Under-promise, over-perform. Deliver, excel. Go the extra mile. Give your cloak when asked for your coat. Do more, be more. Grow out of your problems. Never, never, never quit. Do more than you are asked to do and more than is expected.

5. You cannot rise above your calendar. Show me your calendar, your schedule; show me who you hang out with, and I'll show you your bottom line. Set your priorities, then work at them.

6. Transcend problems. You are bigger than your problems. Find a noble and gracious way to overcome. Sometimes a "time out" is in order. Concentrate on solutions more than on problems. Usually others around you have already come up with the solution; you merely need to find it.

7. Work on your resolve. Bottom line: nothing happens until you complete the work. Most success is accomplished by fortitude and perseverance. When you slip, check your resolve level.

8. Work on your passion. Love what you do. Even the mundane can be fun if you view it that way. As you lift others, you lift yourself. Your income will increase as your passion increases, and you set the tone for your destiny. This applies to all areas of your life.

9. Work. Work hard. Work smart. You figure the ratios, but you must work to be happy. Many think happiness is in relaxing, and although that's necessary, get back to work. We are meant to be busy. Stress is good; it makes us perform better.

10. Do frequent attitude checks. You are "You, Incorporated." You're the president, vice president, secretary, and treasurer. You are the board of directors. With so much control, can you risk having a bad attitude? Be a "honing" signal to yourself. Stay on track.

11. Walk a lot. Every major thinker, including Jesus, walked everywhere. It's great for the body, but better for the brain. It also works wonders on our psyche.

12. Love your family and friends. Involve them. Have frequent councils. Be unattached to the uncontrollable aspects of your business or career, but be very attached to your loved ones.

13. Do extraordinary things. When your competitors are sleeping, what are you doing? Mediocrity inspires no one. The pursuit of excellence will get the A-pluses.

14. Do layups. I'm impressed when I see multimillion dollar basketball players doing layups. Do the basics every day. Yes, they are mundane, sometimes trivial, but they are sine qua non to success. You can add the wild, the exotic, and the spectacular as you go.

15. Be creative. Solve problems; brainstorm. Think things through. Try and test new ideas. Don't be closed minded. Live a serendipitous life. Be a "what else would I do?" person.

16. Seek peace. I know this sounds strange here, but while the busy-ness has its place, and the achieving and doing are important, there is a need to have peace. "Be still, and know that I *am* GOD." (Psalm 46:10)

¹⁷ *And the work of righteousness shall be peace; and the effect of righteousness quietness and assurance for ever.*

¹⁸ *And my people shall dwell in a peaceable habitation, and in sure dwellings, and in quiet resting places;*

Isaiah 32:17, 18

17. Do good. Go about doing good. Look for opportunities to help others. Do well in your work so you can do good at all times.

18. Live a life of abundance. Develop an abundance of faith and good will. Have an abundance of patience. Study, learn, and apply wise practices. Eliminate scarcity; it's not God's way. Prosperity and abundance are.

I'm impressed when I see happy, healthy people. It's contagious. They are always doing things. At the first part of this book I wrote about enthusiasm. It is necessary for success. We can't take shortcuts to Heaven. We also can't cheat success. We have to be real.

Being real means living a life of integrity. It's not hard. Just make sure that what you *think, say, do,* and *are* are the same.

I've given methods to get on track and keep on track—to build and keep our resolve. I've explored the giving and forgiving process and the wonderful miracles found walking down that path.

I hope you have enjoyed this book. In conclusion, I wanted to write something spectacular. Something earth-shattering, something that you will remember forever. For weeks, I drew a mental blank. Then one early morning it came to me. Go again to the scriptures. Look up the word "finish" in your word search program.

That's it. I know it's not earth-shaking, but it is so vital, so important. Look at the wonderful words of Jesus at the Last Supper:

⁴   *I have glorified thee on the earth: I have finished*
     the work which thou gavest me to do.

John 17:4

He finished the work. He completed the job. No questions asked and no excuses. He came to do the work of His Father and He finished it.

There are so many starters, so many who begin the race, but so few who finish. Why? Probably because they didn't realize the sacrifices needed. They did not calculate the cost.

> 28 *For which of you, intending to build a tower, sitteth not down first, and counteth the cost, whether he have sufficient to finish it?*
> 29 *Lest haply, after he hath laid the foundation, and is not able to finish it, all that behold it begin to mock him,*
> 30 *Saying, This man began to build, and was not able to finish.*
>
> *Luke 14:28-30*

By the way, a few verses later, Jesus tells us that the cost is to be willing to forsake all and follow Him.

These words are so powerful. Take the first step. Don't stop. Let these words be a guide. Do you have what it takes to finish the job? If not, recalculate, refigure. Get what it takes or do something else. Look at the apostle Paul's words:

> 24 *But none of these things move me, neither count I my life dear unto myself, so that I might finish my course with joy.*
>
> *Acts 20:24*

We, too, must be finishers. All else is meaningless unless we finish.

Look at the Lord Jesus' very last words on the earth.

> 30 *When Jesus therefore had received the vinegar, he said, 'It is finished': and he bowed his head and gave up the ghost.*
>
> *John 19:30*

101

I'm so grateful He finished His work. Because of Him, I have hope. Because of Him, I strive every day to live better.

We all are on an important trek through life. Our choice is simple. Do we fill our lives with the good, the noble, and, to all extent possible, the divine? Or do we fill it with the ugly, the dross, and the mediocre?

The choice is ours, and we get to live out our choice every day. Change now. Do good works, so when we report back we, like Paul, can say, "I've finished the course."

Take frequent doses of God's word. You can't take enough vitamin C on January first to last the whole year. Likewise, God's words need to be in daily doses. Remember, be a doer of God's words, not just a hearer.

Available Resources

Lighthouse Publishing Group, Inc. or Wade Cook Seminars, Inc. staff have reviewed the following books and educational materials. They are suggested as reading and resource materials to help you lead a richer life. Because new ideas and techniques come along and laws change, we're always updating our resource list. To order a copy of our current resource catalogue, please write or call us at:

Lighthouse Publishing Group, Inc.
14675 Interurban Avenue South
Seattle, Washington 98168-4664
1-800-706-8657

Or, visit us on our websites at:
www.lighthousebooks.com

The following books are available in better bookstores everywhere. To order any other products, please call our toll free number: 800-872-7411. Also, we would love to hear your comments about our products and services, as well as your success stories. Please send these to Lighthouse Publishing Group, Inc. at the above address. As a special thank you, we'll send you a free gift. Be sure to mention offer code AR98 when you write! We look forward to hearing from you!

Books

General Finance

Brilliant Deductions
By Wade B. Cook

Do you want to make the most of the money you earn? Do you want to have solid tax havens and ways to reduce the taxes you pay? Then *Brilliant Deductions* is for you! Learn to structure yourself and your family for tax savings and liability protection and discover how to get (and stay) rich in spite of the new tax laws.

Blueprints for Success, Volume I
Contributors: Joel Black, JJ Childers, Wade Cook, Keven Hart, Debbie Losse, Tim Semingson, Dan Wagner, Dave Wagner, Steve Wirrick, Gregory Witt, and Rich Simmons.

Blueprints For Success is a compilation of the thoughts and tips of 11 incredibly successful people. Like a builder uses blueprints to construct a building, this book will provide the necessary guidance for you to build a successful life. In *Blueprints For Success, Vol. I*, the authors explore what it takes to succeed, as well as teach basic stock market strategies for financial success. You'll learn how to train your mind to succeed, how to live today for a successful tomorrow, how to find financial success in the stock market as a whole, specific strategies for stock market success that require little money, and how to keep yourself successful.

Wade Cook's Power Quotes
By Wade B. Cook

Wade Cook's Power Quotes is chock full of exciting quotes that have motivated and inspired Mr. Cook. Wade Cook continually asks his students, "To whom are you listening?" He knows that if you get your advice and inspiration from successful people, you'll become successful yourself. He compiled *Wade Cook's Power Quotes* to provide you with a millionaire-on-call when you need advice.

Wealth 101
By Wade B. Cook

This incredible book brings you 101 strategies for wealth creation and protection that you can't afford to miss. Front to back, it is packed full of tips and tricks to supercharge your financial health. If you need to generate more cash flow, *Wealth 101* shows you several possible avenues. If you are already wealthy, *Wealth 101* shows you strategy upon strategy for decreasing your tax liability and increasing your peace of mind through liability protection.

Million-Heirs
By John V. Childers, Jr.

In his reader-friendly style, attorney John V. Childers, Jr. explains how you can prepare your loved ones for when you pass away. He explains many details you need to take care of right away, before a death occurs, as well as strategies for your heirs to utilize. Don't leave your loved ones unprepared, get *Million-Heirs*.

Secret Millionaire Guide To Nevada Corporations
By John V. Childers, Jr.

What does it mean to be a secret millionaire? In *Secret Millionaire Guide To Nevada Corporations*, attorney John V. Childers, Jr. outlines exactly how you can use some of the secret, extraordinary business tactics used by many of today's super-wealthy to protect your assets from the ravages of lawsuits and other destroyers, using Nevada Corporations. You'll understand why the state of Nevada has become the preferred jurisdiction for those desiring to establish corporations and how to utilize Nevada Corporations for your financial benefit.

Lifestyle Enhancement
Business Buy The Bible
By Wade B. Cook

Inspired by the Creator, the Bible truly is the authority for running the business of life. Throughout *Business Buy The Bible*, you are provided with practical advice that helps you apply God's word to your life. You'll learn how you can apply God's words to saving, spending and investing, and how you can control debt instead of being controlled by it. You'll also learn how to use God's principles in your daily business activities and prosper.

Don't Set Goals
By Wade B. Cook

Don't Set Goals will teach you to be a goal-getter, not just a goal-setter. You'll learn that achieving goals is the result of prioritizing and acting. *Don't Set Goals* shows you how taking action and "paying the price" is more important than simply making the decision to do something. Don't just set goals. Go out and get your goals, go where you want to go!

Living In Color
By Renae Knapp

Renae Knapp is the leading authority on the Blue Base/Yellow Base Color System and is recognized worldwide for her research and contribution to the study of color. Industries, universities, and men and women around the globe use Renae's tried and true—scientifically proven—system to achieve measurable results.

In *Living In Color*, Renae Knapp teaches you easy to understand methods which empower you to get more from your life by harnessing the power of color. In an engaging, straightforward way, Renae Knapp teaches the scientific Blue Base/Yellow Base Color System and how to achieve harmony and peace using color. You will develop a mastery of color harmony and an awareness of the amazing role color plays in every area of your life.

Real Estate

101 Ways To Buy Real Estate Without Cash
By Wade B. Cook

101 Ways To Buy Real Estate Without Cash is the book for the investor who wants innovative and practical methods for buying real estate with little or no money down. If you want to increase your profits, you need to read this book.

Cook's Book On Creative Real Estate
By Wade B. Cook

Make your real estate buying experiences profitable *and* fun. *Cook's Book On Creative Real Estate* will show you how! You will learn suggestions for finding the right properties, buying them quickly, and profiting even quicker.

How To Pick Up Foreclosures
By Wade B. Cook

How To Pick Up Foreclosures shows you how to buy real estate at 60¢ on the dollar or less. You'll learn to find houses before you go to the foreclosure auction and purchase them with no bank financing. *How To Pick Up Foreclosures* takes Wade's methods from *Real Estate Money Machine* and super charges them by applying the fantastic principles to already-discounted properties.

Owner Financing
By Wade B. Cook

This is a short but invaluable booklet you can give to sellers who hesitate to owner finance. Let this pamphlet convince both you and them that owner financing is the *only* way to buy and sell real estate.

Real Estate For Real People
By Wade B. Cook

A priceless, comprehensive overview of real estate investing, *Real Estate For Real People* teaches you how to buy the right property, for the right price, at the right time. Mr. Cook explains all of the strategies you'll need, and shows you why and how to invest in real estate. You can retire rich with real estate, and have fun doing it!

Real Estate Money Machine
By Wade B. Cook

Wade's first best selling book reveals the secrets of Wade Cook's own system—the system he earned his first million from. *Real Estate Money Machine* teaches you how to make money regardless of the state of the economy. Wade's innovative concepts for investing in real estate not only avoids high interest rates, but avoids banks altogether.

Stock Market

Bear Market Baloney

By Wade B. Cook

A more timely book wouldn't be possible. Wade's predictions came true while the book was at press! Don't miss this insightful look into what makes bull and bear markets and how to make exponential returns in any market.

Rolling Stocks

By Gregory Witt

Rolling Stocks shows you the simplest and most powerful strategy for profiting from the ups and down of the stock market. You'll learn how to find rolling stocks, get in smoothly at the right price, and time your exit. You will recognize the patterns of rolling stocks and how to make the most money from these strategies. Apply rolling stock principles to improve your trading options and fortify your portfolio.

Sleeping Like A Baby

By John C. Hudelson

Perhaps the most predominant reason people don't invest in the stock market is fear. *Sleeping Like A Baby* removes the fear from investing and gives you the confidence and knowledge to invest wisely, safely, and profitably.

You'll learn how to build a high quality portfolio and plan for your future and let your investments follow. Begin to invest as early as possible, and use proper asset allocation and diversification to reduce risk.

Stock Market Miracles

By Wade B. Cook

The eagerly anticipated partner to *Wall Street Money Machine*, this book is proven to be just as invaluable. *Stock Market Miracles* improves on some of the strategies from *Wall Street Money Machine* and introduces new and valuable twists on our old favorites. This must read, a *New York Times* Business Best Seller, is for anyone interested in making serious money in the stock market.

Wall Street Money Machine
By Wade B. Cook

Appearing on the *New York Times* Business Best Sellers list for two years, *Wall Street Money Machine* contains the best strategies for wealth enhancement and cash flow creation in the stock market. Throughout *Wall Street Money Machine*, Wade Cook describes 11 of his proven strategies for generating cash flow using the stock market. It's a great primer for creating wealth using the Wade Cook stock market strategies.

Home Study Courses

Free Cassettes

Income Formulas—A free cassette
By Wade B. Cook

Preview the 11 cash flow strategies taught in the Wall Street Workshop.

Income Streams—A free cassette
By Wade B. Cook

Learn to buy and sell real estate quickly and profitably using the Wade Cook method.

Money Mysteries of the Millionaires—A free cassette
By Wade B. Cook

Learn how to use personal Nevada Corporations, Living Trusts, Pension Plans, Charitable Remainder Trusts, and Family Limited Partnerships to protect your assets.

Power Of Nevada Corporations—A free cassette
By Wade B. Cook

The Power of Nevada Corporations tape teaches you how to maximize the privacy, reduced taxes, and protect your assets with Nevada Corporations.

Audiocassettes

Financial Fortress
By Wade B. Cook

This eight-part home study course is the last word in entity structuring. It goes far beyond mere financial planning or estate planning to help you structure your business and your affairs to reduce taxes, retire rich, escape lawsuits, bequeath your assets without government interference, and, in short, bombproof your entire estate.

High Performance Business Strategies
By Wade B. Cook

Wade Cook and his staff have listened to people's questions and concerns for decades, and they know that business problems are best solved by people who already know the ropes. Unfortunately, those people can be difficult to find when you need answers. To make it easy for you to get help when you need it, Wade Cook Seminars, Inc. staff categorized the most common business questions and came up with about 60 major areas of concern. Wade then went into the recording studio and dealt head on with these issues. What resulted is a comprehensive collection of knowledge to help you succeed quickly.

Money Machine I & II
By Wade B. Cook

Learn the benefits of buying and, more importantly, selling real estate. The proven, effective system for creating and maintaining a real estate money machine is now available on audiocassettes. Money Machine I & II teach the step-by-step cash flow formulas that made Wade Cook, and thousands like him, successful real estate investors.

Paper Tigers and Paper Chase
By Wade B. Cook

In six informative audiocassettes, Mr. Cook shares his inside secrets for establishing a cash flow business with real estate investments. You'll learn how to find discounted mortgages, as well as how you can get 40% plus yields on your money. Learn the art of structuring your business to attract investors and bring in a desirable income through family corporations, pension plans, and other legal entities. A detailed manual is included to help you get started. As a bonus, when you buy Paper Tigers you'll also receive Paper Chase for free. Paper Chase holds the most important tools you need to make deals happen.

Retirement Prosperity
By Wade B. Cook

Take your IRA money and invest it in ways that generate you bigger, better, and quicker returns! This four tape set walks you through a system for using a self directed IRA to create phenomenal profits, virtually tax free! This is one of the most complete systems for IRA investing ever created; don't be without it!

Unlimited Wealth
By Wade B. Cook

Unlimited Wealth is the "University of Money-Making Ideas" home study course that helps you improve your finances. The heart and soul of this seminar teaches how to make more money, pay fewer taxes, and keep more money for your retirement and family.

Zero To Zillions
By Wade B. Cook

This powerful workshop on Wall Street helps you understand the stock market game, play it successfully, and retire rich. Learn 11 powerful investment strategies to avoid pitfalls and losses, catch Day-trippers, Bottom fish, write Covered Calls, double your money in one week with options on stock split companies, and so much more.

Videos

Build Perpetual Income (BPI)

Build Perpetual Income is the latest in our ever-expanding series of real estate seminar home study courses. In this video, you will learn powerful real estate cash-flow generating techniques, including: power negotiating strategies, buying and selling mortgages, writing contracts, finding and buying discount properties, and avoiding debt.

Dynamic Dollars Video
By Wade B. Cook

Dynamic Dollars is Wade Cook's 90-minute introduction to the basics of his stock market strategies. Mr. Cook explains the meter drop philosophy, Rolling Stock, Proxy Investing, and writing Covered Calls. It's perfect for anyone looking for information on making incredible returns.

Wall Street Workshop Video Series
By Wade B. Cook

If you can't make it to the Wall Street Workshop soon, get a head start with these videos. This series is comprised of ten videos containing 11 hours of intense instruction on Rolling Stock, options, stock split companies, writing Covered Calls, and seven other tested and proven strategies designed to help you increase the value of your investments.

Next Step Video Series
By Team Wall Street

This advanced version of the Wall Street Workshop is full of power-packed stock market strategies from Wade Cook. This is not a duplicate of the Wall Street Workshop, but a vital follow-up. The methods taught in the Next Step Video Series supercharge the strategies taught in the Wall Street Workshop and teach you even more ways to make more money!

Seminars

Cook University

People enroll in **Cook University** for a variety of reasons. Usually they are a little discontented with where they are— their job is not working, their business is not producing the kind of income they want, or they definitely see that they need more income to prepare for a better retirement. That's where **Cook University** comes in. As you try to live the American Dream, in the lifestyle you want, we are ready to teach you how you can make your dreams a reality.

You can't afford to miss this training. The number to call is 1-800-872-7411. Call right away! Perpetual monthly income is waiting. We'll teach you how to achieve it. We'll show you how to make it. We'll watch over you while you're making it happen. If you want to be wealthy, Cook University is the place to be.

Business Entity Skills Training (BEST)
Presented by Wade B. Cook and the Gold Team

Our entity planners will help you learn and use six powerful entities to protect your wealth and your family. Learn the secrets of asset protection, eliminate your fear of litigation, and minimize your taxes.

Executive Retreat
Presented by Wade B. Cook and Team Wall Street

Created especially for the individuals already owning or planning to establish Nevada Corporations, the Executive Retreat is a unique opportunity for corporate executives to participate in workshops geared toward streamlining operations and maximizing efficiency and impact.

Wall Street Workshop
Presented by Wade B. Cook and Team Wall Street

The Wall Street Workshop teaches you how to make incredible money in all stock markets. It teaches you the tried-and-true strategies that have made hundreds of people wealthy.

113

Next Step Workshop
Presented by Wade B. Cook and Team Wall Street

This is an advanced Wall Street Workshop designed to help those ready to take their trading to the next level and treat it as a business. This seminar is open only to graduates of the Wall Street Workshop.

Real Estate Workshop
Presented by Wade B. Cook and Team Main Street

The Real Estate Workshop teaches you how to build perpetual income for life. The topics include buying and selling paper, finding discounted properties, generating long-term monthly cash flow, and controlling properties without owning them.

Real Estate BootCamp
Presented by Wade B. Cook and Team Main Street

This three or four-day BootCamp is truly a roll-up-your-sleeves-and-do-the-deals event. You will learn to locate bargains, negotiate strategies, and find wholesale properties. You will also visit a title company, look at properties, and learn new and fun selling strategies.

Wealth Institute
Presented by Wade B. Cook and the Gold Team

This three-day workshop defines the art of asset protection and entity planning. You'll learn the six domestic entities that protect you from lawsuits, taxes, and financial losses, and help you retire rich.

Resources

IQ Pager™

If you're getting your financial information from the evening news, you're getting it too late. IQ Pager™ is a paging system that alerts you as events and announcements are made on Wall Street. With IQ Pager™, you receive instant information about major stock split announcements, earnings surprises, important mergers and acquisitions, judgements or court decisions, important bankruptcy announcements, big winners and losers, and more.

Idea Exchange
By Lighthouse Publishing

The *Idea Exchange* program is a reading and study guide designed to assist you in understanding and implementing the strategies and ideas found in Lighthouse Publishing Group's books. At bookstores all over the country, and on line at lighthousebooks.com, Lighthouse Publishing Group, Inc. provides a forum for people to learn and grow together, an opportunity for readers to exchange their ideas and experiences and a way to improve your finances through education. As a member of the Idea Exchange reading group, you, along with other investors, will share investment experiences through workbooks and real-life activities.

Legal Forms
By Wade B. Cook

This is a collection of pertinent legal forms used in real estate transactions. These forms were selected by experienced investors and are essential to help you keep on top of your personal investing.

Record Keeping System
By Wade B. Cook

This is a complete record keeping system for organizing all of the information on each of your real estate investments. The Record Keeping System keeps track of everything from insurance policies to equity growth. You will know at a glance exactly where you stand with your investment properties and you will sleep better at night.

Travel Agent Information
By John Childers and Wade B. Cook

Travel Agent Information is the only sensible solution for the frequent traveler. This kit includes all of the information and training you need to be a contract travel agent for a reliable travel company. There are no hassles, no requirements, and no forms or restrictions, just all the benefits of traveling for substantially less every time.

Wealth Information Network (W.I.N.)™

This subscription internet service provides you with the latest financial formulas and updated entity structuring strategies. New, timely information is entered Monday through Friday, sometimes four or five times a day. Wade Cook and his Team Wall Street staff write for W.I.N.™, giving you updates on their own current stock plays, companies who announced earnings, companies who announced stock splits, and the latest trends in the market.